PUTNAM COUNTY COURTHOUSE
OTTAWA, OHIO

COMMEMORATING 100 YEARS
1913-2013

by

Randall L. Basinger
Putnam County Common Pleas Judge

and

Roselia Deters Verhoff
former Putnam County Auditor

Produced by
Nancy Kline

September 2013

CONTENTS

Preface

I. Establishing Putnam County 1

II. The Petition 7

III. The Vote 12

IV. Building Commission and Architect 13

V. Controversy 16

VI. Plans to Begin Construction 18

VII. Construction Moves Forward 20

VIII. Construction Nears Completion 21

IX. Correlation to the Narrative
    01. Preliminary Studies and Sketches 22
    02. Elected Official 25
    03. 'Putnam County Courthouse Built' 26
    04. Second Floor Corridor 27
    05. Interior of Principal Courtroom 28
    06. Extensive Marble 29
    07. Construction Continued 30
    08. Ornamental Wall and Ceiling Plastering 31
    09. Lumber and Interior Finish 32
    10. Sky Lights and Stained Glass 33
    11. Flood of 1913 34

X. Court House History Comes to Life Through Memories 35

XI History Panels Traveling Exhibit 51

XII Epilogue 77
XIII Pictures from the Past 78
XIV Court House Pictures 82

PREFACE

Putnam County, Ohio was platted in 1820 and was organized in 1834 when county officials were appointed/elected. In its history there have been two county seats and four courthouses. Kalida was the first county seat and two courthouses were built in that village. Ottawa is the second county seat. Its 1867 two-story red brick building was replaced in 1909-1913. In 2013 we commemorate the 100th anniversary of this courthouse.

Court House Centennial Commission
Named by Commissioners

Resolution

The Board of County Commissioners of Putnam County, Ohio met in regular session on the 7th day of February, 2013, at the office of said Board with the following members present: Mr. Travis A. Jerwers, Mr. Vincent T. Schroeder, and Mr. John E. Love.

Mr. Jerwers moved the adoption of the following resolution:

Whereas, The Putnam County Court House located at 245 E. Main Street, Ottawa, Ohio will be 100 years old this year as construction was completed in 1913, and

Whereas, In celebration of the centennial, the Board of County Commissioners deems it necessary to name a centennial commission to plan for the dedication and celebration of the 100th anniversary, now therefore, be it

Resolved, The Board of County Commissioners does hereby name the following to plan the dedication and celebration of the 100th anniversary of the Putnam County Court House:

Judge Randall Basinger, Putnam County Common Pleas Judge
Roselia Verhoff, local historian and former Putnam County auditor
Teresa Lammers, Putnam County Clerk of Courts
Cathy Recker, Putnam County Recorder
John Love, Putnam County Commissioner

Mr. Schroeder seconded the motion and the roll being called upon its adoption, the vote resulted as follows:

Signed:
John E. Love, Yes
Vincent T. Schroeder, Yes
Travis A. Jerwers, Yes
BOARD OF COUNTY COMMISSIONERS
PUTNAM COUNTY, OHIO

Attest: *Betty Schroeder*
Betty Schroeder, Clerk

The Centennial Commission held its first meeting on April 4, 2013. At that time other citizens were invited to help plan the centennial commemoration: local historians Nancy Kline, Ruth Wilhelm, Bruce Stowe, and Betty Wannemacher. Additional photographs were contributed by Eric Wilhelm and Becky Leader.

I. ESTABLISHING PUTNAM COUNTY, OHIO

The County's Heritage

Call the roll of Ohio's eighty-eight counties and Putnam will answer to the name of a Revolutionary War officer. General Israel Putnam (1718-1790) served in the Revolutionary War as a part of George Washington's Continental Army. General Putnam, who survived fighting the French and Indians, fought in the Battle of Bunker Hill.

Putnam County was twenty-four miles square when it was created in 1820 as a political subdivision of the State of Ohio. This old Indian Territory was a part of the Great Black Swamp that once covered much of the county. The swamp was 30 to 40 miles wide and ran for 120 miles from the Sandusky River on the east to Fort Wayne, Indiana on the west.

In 1829 the State Legislature appointed a commission to locate and name a county seat. Kalida, believed to be the center of population at the time, was selected. This village in Union Township was near Plum Creek and Sugar Creek, and was adjacent to the Ottawa River on its west side. Although the county was created (boundaries established) earlier it did not function as an autonomous county until it was organized (office holders appointed/elected).

In 1834 Governor Robert Lucas commissioned William Cochran, Henry Morris, and Silas McClish as Associate Judges of the Putnam County Court

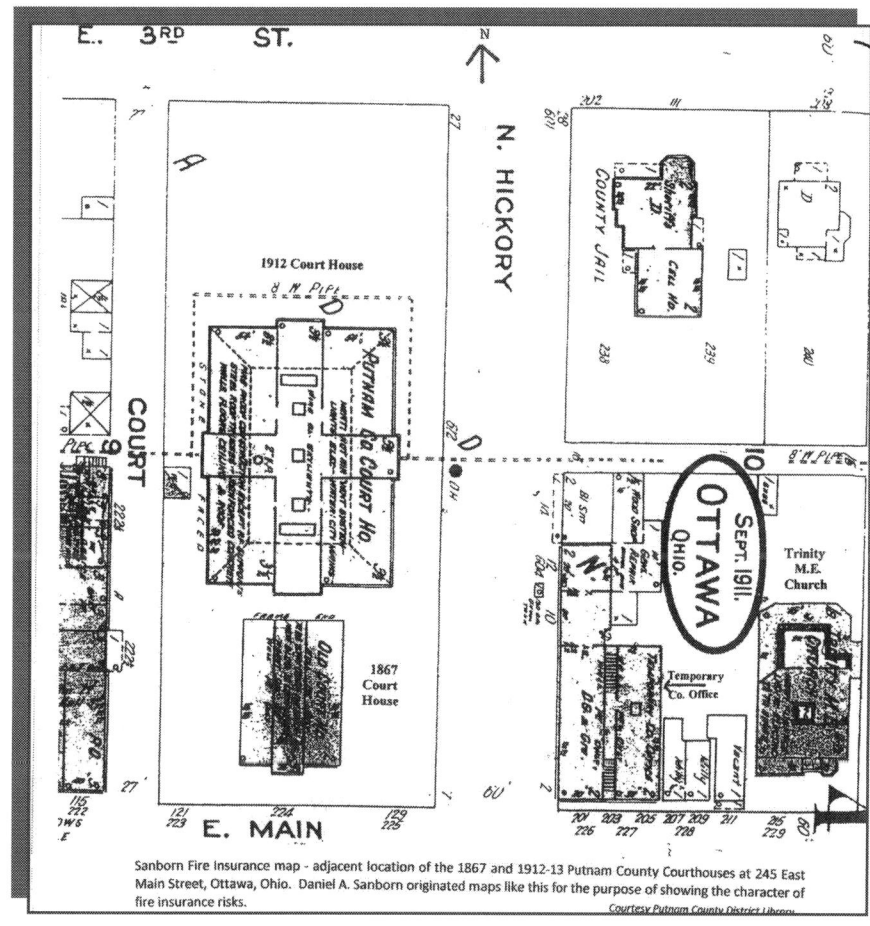

Sanborn Fire Insurance map - adjacent location of the 1867 and 1912-13 Putnam County Courthouses at 245 East Main Street, Ottawa, Ohio. Daniel A. Sanborn originated maps like this for the purpose of showing the character of fire insurance risks.
Courtesy Putnam County District Library

of Common Pleas. These three men were charged with the responsibility of officially organizing the county. When the Associate Judges met in May 1834 at the home of Abraham Sarber, Kalida, they elected Daniel W. Gray as Clerk and Amos Evans as Prosecuting Attorney. They appointed Thomas Gray, Samuel Myers, and William Priddy as County Commissioners and Ferdinand C. Fitch as County Surveyor. When they met again in August 1834 at the home of Abraham Sarber they appointed William Cochran as Sheriff and William Turner as Coroner. The election in October 1834 for commissioners, an auditor, treasurer, sheriff, coroner, recorder, and surveyor finalized the county's organization.

Court Houses at Kalida

A temporary frame structure, built about 1835, housed the offices of the county officials until it was replaced in 1839 by a "stately" brick Court House. In the winter of 1862 a fire in the Recorder's office damaged and destroyed many of the records. The Court House was again struck by fire in the winter of 1864, this time so severe that the building was declared unusable. Smaller buildings were placed on the Court House grounds and the business of county continued.

In December 1864 County Commissioners John Deffenbaugh, Conrad Henry, and Simon Maple called a meeting to discuss the condition of the county's business buildings. "Propositions for repairing or rebuilding the Court House were discussed before them, good-humoredly but with animation, from several standpoints of Kalida, Ottawa, and Columbus Grove [residents]." The Board asked for proposals, to be received at their next regular meeting, to repair the ruins of the Court House "so recently tried by fire." *(Kalida Sentinel* December 29, 1864)

Early in 1865 the question arose - should the county seat remain at Kalida or be removed to another location? Some occurrences may have generated this question. In 1848 the county decreased in size when 114 sections were detached from its south side when Auglaize County was created. This change in area may have affected the perceived center of the county. By 1858 the Baltimore and Ohio Railroad passed through Columbus Grove, Ottawa, Leipsic, and Belmore and provided an additional means of transportation.

In February 1865 the Ohio State Legislature considered an enabling bill that would have permitted an election to determine if the county seat should be relocated. The bill was defeated in the Legislature so the Board of Commissioners proceeded to make plans for rebuilding in Kalida.

In an attempt to recover records destroyed in the Court House fire, the following item appeared in the *Kalida Sentinel:*

Notice - To Owners of Land in Putnam County: The Auditor's transfer book having been consumed in the burning of the Court House, persons having deeds transferred during the year 1864 prior to the burning, will be under the necessity of bringing in their deeds and have them retransferred, otherwise the lands must of necessity remain in the names of the original owners. Samuel P. Weaver, Auditor Putnam County - April 6, 1865.

How many deeds were re-recorded after this announcement was published is unknown. The County Commissioners covered the cost of having these legal documents duplicated in the Recorder's books.

In July 1865 James L. Olney, Milton C. Ewing, Jacob Bressler, Thomas H. B. Hipkins, Cortes Ewing, Samuel Shoup, Mathew C. Ewing, Lewis E. Holtz, Calvin T. Pomeroy, and Bernard Leopold, as plaintiffs, filed a petition in the Court of Common Pleas praying for an injunction to be issued against County Commissioners Conrad Henry, Simon Maple, and Herman H. Recker; Treasurer Nelson H. McCracken, and Auditor Samuel P. Weaver, Putnam County; and David Lloyd of William Keplinger and Company, and S. P. Havil and Company, to restrain them from proceeding to rebuild the Court House at Kalida.

The plaintiffs' contention was that the county commissioners were restricted from spending more than $5,000.00 "without submitting the question as to the policy of such expenditure to the qualified voters of the county, as they are required by law to do so." Both parties argued the pros and cons of the case before Judge O. W. Rose at Lima. The judge granted the injunction.

The defendants served notice on the plaintiffs' attorney that a motion would be made to Judge Conklin of Sidney to dissolve the injunction. The attorneys on both sides were on hand on August 3, 1865, but "for some unaccountable reason the Judge was not. Consequently the injunction did not dissolve."

Again a notice was sent that the motion would be heard before the District Court of Wyandot County, Upper Sandusky, on August 17, 1865. The Court refused to hear the motion. The injunction remained in force.

On September 16, 1865 an announcement appeared in the *Kalida Sentinel*, over the names of W. W. Williams, John B. Fruchey, Noah W. Ogan, Day and McHenry, Jacob Gessell, and Albert Postelwait. It read:

Notice is hereby given that there will be a petition presented to the Legislature of the State of Ohio, at their next annual session, praying for the removal of the county seat of Putnam County from Kalida to Columbus Grove, in said county.

County Seat Relocation

The Ohio Senate and the Ohio House of Representatives passed an enabling act in the spring of 1866 that allowed for an election concerning the location of the Putnam County seat of government. This ordinance established the means whereby the matter could be placed before the electorate. In October 1866 two choices appeared on the general election ballot for location of the county seat - Kalida and Ottawa. The total vote, published in the *Putnam County Sentinel* on October 11, 1866, was 3,144 with 1,908 voting for relocation to Ottawa and 1,236 voting to have the county seat remain in Kalida.

County Records Moved East

The question arose about moving county records to the new county seat where no Court House yet existed. The County Commissioners decided to postpone the transfer of records because court was called for Kalida on October 23rd and the subpoenas and summonses of witnesses and jurors had already been made out for their appearance at Kalida. The court adjourned on the 23rd and then reconvened in Ottawa on October 24th.

When the court moved to Ottawa it met in the Methodist Evangelical Church, then located at 321 East Main Street, until the new courtrooms were ready. The annual report for the fiscal year 1866, by the Board of Commissioners to the Court of Common Pleas, listed expenses such as

...paid O. Talburt for windows and door locks broken on church during holding Court,
paid William P. Summers and E. Tracy for cleaning church after March term of Court, paid
Samuel P. Weaver for furnishing sawdust in church preparatory to holding April term of Court
and removal of same.

That same annual report concluded with the statement

During the year six county offices have been built. This together with expenses incurred in
furnishing these offices with the necessary furniture, blank books, together with repairs to
the county safe made necessary by an attack made on it by burglars, and expenses incurred
in moving books, furniture, and other items, and rent paid for offices before completion of
new offices, and also expenses of recording and indexing records made necessary by the
recent fire, and late laws regarding indexing in clerk's office, have necessarily increased the
expenditures much beyond what they otherwise would have been.

In December 1866 entries in the Commissioners Journal listed payments to Samuel P. Weaver, Auditor; Nelson H. McCracken, Treasurer; and James Monroe, Recorder for the expense of moving books and furniture of county offices from Kalida to Ottawa. Rooms in Ottawa were rented from John Fipp, John G. Bookholt, John Beck, Joseph Gerding, and possibly others, for use as temporary county offices.

1867 Court House, Ottawa

By December 1866 the site for the Court House in Ottawa had been decided. It would be built on lots purchased from Dr. Calvin T. Pomeroy near the corner of East Main and North Hickory Streets, in 2013 known as 245 East Main Street. The location was described as "lying west of the Methodist Evangelical Church on Main Cross Street. The site is beautiful, containing three town lots, and in the immediate vicinity of the business part of town." *Putnam County Sentinel,* December 15, 1866.

Before the year ended an announcement appeared in the newspaper.

Notice to Builders. Notice is hereby given that sealed proposals will be received at the Auditor's office in Ottawa, Putnam County, Ohio, until the 22nd day of January 1867 to build a Court House in said town of Ottawa. For plans and specifications, call at the Auditor's office. By order of the Commissioners of Putnam County, Ohio. Samuel P. Weaver, Auditor. *Putnam County Sentinel* December 22, 1866

The bids were opened on the 22nd and

...ranged from $22,000 down to that of Messrs. Enzy and Miller, of this place, which was $17,030. The Commissioners awarded the contract to the above-mentioned firm. There were in all, some thirteen different bids, but a number were conjectured to be by the same firm who took this method to make it, as they supposed, a sure thing. ... The building in size will be seventy-five feet deep--- foundation to be of limestone, walls of brick, two stories high, with cupola, slate roof, and iron cornices. ... The first story will be finished for the different county offices and the second story for court and jury rooms, all in elegant style. Messrs. Enzy and Miller are both men of experience in the building business, the former of masonry and the latter of wood structure. Mr. Enzy, we believe, has at the present time, quite a large amount of brick, which he proposes putting into the walls. The building will be erected during the summer. *Putnam County Sentinel,* January 24, 1867.

Construction on the first Court House in Ottawa started in May 1867 with evacuation for the building's foundation. By late June workmen were laying the brick walls and by mid-July the stonework was completed for the first story with the building taking on an appearance of its own. In August the main walls were completed, and laborers were putting on the slate roof and fitting cornice work on the building. The outside was completed in mid-September. By December all of the county officials were located in their offices in the two-story red brick building.

The total cost for construction of the Court House was $20,576.43. Of this amount Ottawa area residents escrowed $15,000.00 to have the county seat relocated to Ottawa and this investment generated interest of $446.45. The remaining $5,129.98 was raised by taxation.

There was an additional cost of $400 for a bell. The telephone had not yet been invented. Among other things a bell was used to call meetings, convene a jury, or remind citizens of special events - or tragedies. In January 1868 a 1,000-pound bell arrived and soon thereafter it was hung in the Court House tower.

Replace the 1867 Court House?

The building served its intended purpose for nearly 35 years. The 1900s had just begun when talk turned toward building a new, larger Court House.

In the fall of 1902 a topic of conversation in the county concerned replacing the Court House. A petition signed by 500 qualified electors was presented to the Board of County Commissioners asking that the issue of a levy for construction of a new Court House be placed before the voters. The group cited faults about the present structure such as it being insufficient and regarded as unsafe when the second floor court room had large crowds; the vault rooms were too small for the increased number of records of the county; the vaults were constructed of limestone that likely would crack and crumble in case of a severe fire; and the present structure compared unfavorably with other court houses of Northwestern Ohio as to capacity, safety, convenience, and architectural appearance. "In short, a reasonable pride in our county, the safety of our records, adequate room for transaction of public business, all call for a new Court House."

The petition was filed with the Board of County Commissioners in October. The petitioners requested that the Commissioners certify a resolution to the county board of elections that a levy for a new Court House be placed before the voters. Commissioner Ignatius Stechschulte moved the adoption of the resolution by the board and David B. Owens seconded the motion. The third commissioner Samuel Cartwright voted yes on the motion. The amount to be expended was $150,000. The issue appeared on the ballot in November 1902. The levy failed. The count was 1,659 for and 4,017 against the Court House building levy.

The issue again appeared on the ballot in September 1909. The levy passed. The count was 2,825 for and 2,129 against - a majority of 696 votes.

Removal of the 1867 Court House

After construction of a new Court House was assured by a vote of the people, the question of removal of the 1867 building came to the forefront. In March 1912 it went on the auction block with the stipulation that the purchaser had to tear it down and clean up the area. "Squire Mullett, of Liberty Township, made the brick. Will he give as much for them in 1912 as he sold them for in 1866-67? ... How much will you give?" *Putnam County Sentinel* March 22, 1912

The county now had two Court House standing on Court House Square. An article about the 1867 building appeared in the *Putnam County Sentinel* March 29, 1912.

The Old Court House---Brick and Booze to be Sold. Next Saturday the old Court House sells at public auction. ... It is reported that a bottle of good whiskey is in the cornerstone of the old building, placed there when the foundation was laid. In order to buy the building it will be necessary to buy some good whiskey. ... It is reported that several well-to-do citizens are prepared to say to prospective bidders that they will give five to ten dollars for this quart of fifty year old tangle-foot fire water.

The Ohio Wrecking Company, Toledo, bought the 1867 Court House on March 30, 1912. The Board of County Commissioners excluded from the sale "the bell in the tower, vault doors, wash stands, and furniture of every description" and other fixtures. The contract with The Ohio Wrecking Company specified that the purchaser "will remove all material including as much foundation as the purchaser feels fit, but said foundation to be taken out at least one foot below the grade line." Commissioners Journal 18, page 590

As early as April 1910 suggestions were made that perhaps the brick in the 1867 building should be used to build an assembly hall at the fairgrounds. "Perhaps it would be a valued relic 50 years from now, standing on the old fairgrounds." Confirmation of this suggestion came about when some of the red bricks were used to build a secretary office near the entrance of the fairground on East Second Street, Ottawa. That building served the Putnam County Agricultural Society until 1978 when it was replaced by a frame building that continues to serve its purpose in 2013.

The history of the 100-year old Courthouse corroborates the intentions of its Building Commission. *"...We want to give something to those who live after us. In the year A.D. 2000 may our posterity say that 'they builded wiser than they knew'."* Putnam County *Sentinel* February 1910

II. THE PETITION

On August 9, 1909, Putnam County citizens filed a petition seeking a vote for a new courthouse. Prominent citizen Ezra Warren of Liberty Township filed the much talked about petition in the auditor's office with five hundred names of Putnam County qualified electors. The petition contained handwritten pages of names with towns or townships.

Citizens from almost every section of Putnam County put their names on the petition. One stated that the people should have a chance to say whether or not they wanted to build a new courthouse, or rebuild and repair the old one. The County commissioners were to set a date upon which the vote would be taken. An election was already set for a September 7, 1909, primary day and that date was suggested.

The petition provided for a total cost of no more than $250,000 for the building, and provided that the County Commissioners could submit a question for any amount less than that sum. The Putnam Sentinel opined that an oversized building should not be planned or built, but that the old building had no basement and the new one should have a basement. The paper also suggested that the foundation should be constructed above ground level to lessen the danger of floods, and noted that the economy would certainly provide for a $200,000 building to accommodate the county for years to come. The petition had provided a high enough estimate in order to give the Commissioners discretion in the amount to be voted on, but some said that even $300,000 would not be too much for a wealthy county like Putnam to spend.

The vote was to settle the question of whether the County Commissioners should repair the old courthouse or build a new courthouse. A no vote would provide for the repair of the old courthouse.

The $200,000 building was to be paid for in a 20 year period of equal payments and would cost $1.14 on each $1000 real estate valuation. A farmer owning 40 acres valued at $30 per acre would pay about $1.50 per year. Bonds would be sold at a rate of approximately 4% or 5%.

The Sentinel in August of 1909 suggested that citizens were face-to-face with the question of a new courthouse and that the vote should be put to the greatest number of people, the petitioners and voters being adult men, as women did not acquire the right to vote until 1920. The paper pointed out that 'state authorities had ruled that something must be done with the old building and that if any disaster occurs, the County commissioners are personally liable for damage.' The Commissioners indicated that they wished to do what ever the majority of the people wanted, either repairing the old building or building a new building. The newspaper suggested that citizens 'talk it over with their neighbor, use business sense, and use judgment as in everyday affairs', as 'no decent man would criticize any other man for voting his honest opinions.'

The question of location was immediately a topic of discussion. Everyone agreed that 'any town would want the County seat if it were offered', but that the location other than Ottawa cannot be changed by the County Commissioners. The question to be put to the voters was not a change of location but rather 'shall bonds be used and sold and the money used in the building of a new courthouse'. The newspapers made clear that the Commissioners would 'undoubtedly proceed to repair and remodel the old building by putting it in a condition to be approved by the state authorities if the vote were no'. They also acknowledged that some wanted the location changed and continued to state that the courthouse should not have been located in Ottawa at all, but the paper pointed out that 'few if any persons now living are responsible for what was done more than 40 years ago' with the 1866 move from Kalida to Ottawa. The paper suggested that the immediate question was to do what is best for now and that 'men with cool heads and cool judgment will have the most influence in settling the question'. The paper suggested that to have progress in government the citizens should do 'what is best for yourself and your county, strike the average, be fair with both yourself and County, and then vote that when election day comes with no need to apologize'.

Headlines in the Sentinel of August 20th, 1909 continued to discuss the benefits of a new courthouse, with the vote coming in less than three weeks. Tuesday, September 7, 1909 was fixed as the date when citizens would decide whether or not a new courthouse would be erected or the old one remodeled. The amount established by the Commissioners for construction was $200,000., but they pointed out that the full amount may not be necessary. The petition had called for up to $250,000 and the Commissioners decided on the limit of $200,000. The Commissioners also indicated that they would have to spend as much as $10,000 for repair of the old building each year, 'the building being cracked from foundation to the roof'. The Commissioners did not take a clear position on the new construction but put the question to the voters. The campaigning Sentinel suggested that men must be larger than their Township, County, State, and even nation.

One of the repeated arguments in favor of a new courthouse was the safety of community documents. The 1864 fire of the Kalida courthouse followed a previous courthouse fire that destroyed a number of documents, including deeds and other courthouse records. News articles urged voters to 'consider the safety and security of records, deeds, mortgages, wills, marriages and divorces', noting that each one concerns property rights and titles to homes and lands. It was reported that not a single fireproof vault was in the old building and that this situation should not continue.

The Sentinel pointed out that a prominent farmer living several miles west of the county seat was in Ottawa the previous Saturday, and in conversation with a friend said that he did not know whether he was in favor of a new building or not. The safety of the records was discussed. The citizen had inherited some of his land, and when he found out if the court house should burn or the records of the Probate Judge's office be destroyed, he would likely have no sure legal title to his lands and he immediately came to the conclusion that the safety of records was more important than location, or the investment of a few dollars for the cost of a new courthouse.

Another Sentinel story reported that a gentleman, living west of Kalida, said he would be glad to see the County seat put back to where it once was in Kalida, however the current vote was simply a question as to whether money should be spent for a new building or to remodel the old one, and he 'wanted his money in a new one'. Others suggested that those who do not know the condition of the old building should look it over before voting, and every honest man in the County should vote what he believes to be the right and best for all concerned.

The newspapers also pointed out that any juror in the last 10 years could testify to the cracked and dilapidated conditions of the building, and that the jury rooms were without proper ventilation and without proper toilets, emphasizing that the old building had been condemned by state inspectors sworn to do their duty. They acknowledged that the old building 'might stand for a dozen years or fall down or burn down', and other 'courthouses have turned to ashes as citizens in Putnam County were well aware'. The paper also reminded voters of the recent Collingwood school building fire in Cleveland, with dozens of children killed because of similar neglect. Fire escapes would be expensive to upgrade the old building and it was argued that it would also be expensive for farmers to quiet title in land disputes should a loss of records occur.

Newspaper stories suggested that voters should call meetings in their town or township and discuss the matter with friends and neighbors, that 'time was running short as the vote was two weeks from next Tuesday'.

The following newspaper issue was approximately ten days before the vote, and nearly the full front page of the Sentinel was devoted to the courthouse question. The County Commissioners had received an order from the chief inspector of Workshops and Factories of the State of Ohio concerning the inspection of the Putnam County Courthouse on April 8, 1908 with an order to remove, in 'a safe and substantial manner all the decayed defective portions of the entire building, and to discontinue the use of the courtroom second-floor for public assemblies'. This was to be done without delay, and a short time later the Commissioners asked what had to be been done to comply with the order. The prosecuting attorney and one of the commissioners went to Columbus to meet with the chief inspector to seek a more definite order of what would be necessary to repair the old courthouse to satisfy the order. A second order was issued which provided that 'upon re-inspection of the courthouse' the County was to remove and repair decayed and defective portions of the entire building and discontinue the use of the courtroom on the second floor, an order essentially condemning the building by indicating that the entire structure was defective. The report pointed out that the foundation was of insufficient strength to support the building and that the brick work was bulged, cracked, and torn apart. The floors were worn out and loose, plastering was loose and had fallen off, that galvanized iron cortices showed signs of decay, window sashes were poorly fitted, electrical wiring was absolutely dangerous, floors and ceilings were out of level, and the joists suffered from dry rot. The conclusion was no portion of the building was in good condition and that it would be 'an imposition on the taxpayers of the County to permit the Commissioners to repair the old building as it would cost as much as a new building'. The chief inspector also concluded that the old courthouse was poorly lighted, without proper toilet facilities, and needed fireproof vaults. Records were in a hazardous position because of wiring and coal heating stoves placed throughout the building.

The newspapers outlined the question as one of the 'best interests of Putnam County', described as the 'best county in northwestern Ohio, perhaps the best in the state'. They questioned spending a large sum of money for repairs for the old courthouse, and still have an old building, when they could economically build a new one. The paper stated that many property owners have trouble getting their titles because of the Kalida Courthouse fire forty five years before and that another fire would cause additional significant problems, pointing out that a fire in the Cincinnati courthouse resulted in a $100,000 payment to replace abstracts that were destroyed and that records there were still incomplete. The Licking County Courthouse was also destroyed, according to the newspaper, and it was nearly impossible to find a land title. Security of ownership and the potential loss of homes and farmland was clearly the message.

News articles also reviewed the cost of the proposed project. The total valuation of the County from the auditor's books was approximately $12 million. A 40 acre plot of land including buildings was valued at approximately $1200, and an individual would pay a total of $25 towards the cost of the new courthouse. With a 10 year bond this would amount to about $2.50 per year at 4%, $2.80 in the first year and $2.08 in the final 10th year.

The newspapers also described offices required to be in the courthouse, including an infirmary office, and directors of elections and that a 'place needed to be suitable so that citizens knew where to find them', including the prosecuting attorney and school boards. The old courthouse had no available rooms for these individuals.

The newspapers continued to give citizen testimonials, including a Van Buren Township taxpayer arguing that 'the old building was a barn and every citizen in the County should be ashamed of it', and that safety of County records is probably a more important reason to vote yes. However, a Blanchard Township voter pointed out that the old building should be 'good enough for the fellows who wanted to stay in it'. The location of the building continued to be a question of discussion and some did not support the petition because it was located at Ottawa, yet pointed out by the newspaper as the most central and convenient for the taxpayers of the County. The Leipsic Free Press referred to the old courthouse as repairing an old shack.

A Friday newspaper story before the upcoming Tuesday vote once again presented extensive details on the cost of a new courthouse and reasons to support the petition. The question was put as 'yes for the construction of a new courthouse by issuing bonds of $200,000' or 'no to compel the commissioners to rebuild the old courthouse as ordered by the State Inspector of Workshops and Factories'. The old courthouse was then 42 years old and was built with limited cost and now condemned by the state. The paper pointed out that one third of the records, for lack of room, are not stored in vaults and that if destroyed by fire could not be replaced, suggesting that repairs would be a waste of money and a temporary fix. The paper further pointed out that when the present courthouse was built the population of the county was small and that number had grown significantly as a 'wealthy County owning some 300,000 acres of the best farmland in the state with 20 thriving villages'. The newspaper computed that 5% bonds payable at $10,000 per year for 20 year period would provide for a payment of $.62 per $1000 assessment.

The newspaper also pointed out the increase in population of the county, with the 1860 census showing a population of 12,808 and the 1910 census being approximately 36,000, suggesting that 'we should not be lagging behind our neighboring counties who all have modern courthouses'. The paper also explained that the Common Pleas Judge would appoint a commission of four, two Democrats and two Republicans to assist the commissioners, and act with them to build a new courthouse. The article also argued that building material was 25% cheaper than it was two years before and that this was a good time to build.

III. The Vote

Putnam Sentinel headline
September 12, 1909
'New Courthouse—YES
Bond issue carries by Big Majority. Taxpayers outside
of the town of Ottawa carried it through.
Now let economy be the watchword'

The voters of Putnam County settled the issue in an 'expression of free men', according to the Putnam County Sentinel days after the vote. The paper pledged to guard against waste and to protect the interests of the taxpayers as the building was constructed, stressing that the cost must be kept under $200,000 as exceeding this limitation was the reason that some citizens were hesitant to support the proposition.

While the Sentinel touted that the issue was supported in distant parts of the county as well as those within the county seat, the vote totals show a slightly different story, with only two of 190 voters in the Village of Kalida supporting the new Courthouse and only 18 of 183 voters in Union Township supporting the construction. The paper did point out that if the vote in the town of Ottawa was eliminated, the bond issue still would have passed.

The paper also pointed out that tactics used by those opposed to a new building 'turned some voters in favor of the project', and that the days are past when 'bulldozing wins in Putnam County'. The newspaper wrote that this aspect of the election needed to be addressed, criticizing anonymous written statements handed out in circulars hours before the election, which included remarks that the Commissioners and Judge Bailey were corrupt and dishonest, and would willfully deceive and betray the people of the county and would permit the stealing of $500,000. The Sentinel pointed out that there was 'never a more dastardly, insinuating charge circulated in this county' than this printed unsigned statement. The circular had pointed out in bold type that $700,000 would likely be spent of the people's money without benefit of law. The paper asked who would say that the Commissioners or Judge Bailey would do such a thing, noting that 'the author of this circular is a coward and should ask for forgiveness or make good his charges', that such 'insults and slanders were about decent people and such rot could help no cause'. The circular had also suggested that the eventual cost would take '3 acres out of every 40 acres of land', perverting the facts and suggesting that the author should be heartily ashamed of himself.

THE OFFICIAL VOTE.

The following is the official vote cast for and against the issuing of bonds:

Twps. & Prec'ts	Yes	No
Blanchard	148	49
Gilboa Corp.	47	13
Greensburg	105	54
Jackson	45	153
Jennings	172	90
Jennings Corps.	57	11
Liberty, E P	63	55
Liberty, W P	79	38
West Leipsic Corp.	30	16
Monroe	49	94
Continental Corp.	63	80
Monterey	123	56
Ottoville Corp.	85	8
Ottawa, E P	119	12
Ottawa Corp. N P	241	4
Ottawa Corp. S P	347	5
Ottawa, W P	76	13
Glandorf Corp.	109	11
Palmer, N P	35	32
Palmer, S P	26	28
Miller City Corp.	33	20
Perry, N P	20	19
Perry, S P	32	62
Dupont Corp.	26	28
Cloverdale Corp.	31	7
Pleasant, N P	109	17
Pleasant, S P	24	48
Col Grove Corp, N P	32	120
Col Grove Corp, S P	44	98
Riley	131	67
Pandora Corp.	66	29
Sugar Creek	59	169
Union	18	165
Kalida Corp.	2	188
Van Buren, N P	33	29
Van Buren, S P	87	44
Leipsic Corp, A	37	96
Leipsic Corp, B	43	84
Belmore Corp	28	16
Totals	**2825**	**2129**
Majority Yes	696	

The official vote shown above was to issue the bonds and to build a new courthouse

IV. Building Commission and Architect

By the week after the vote it seemed that everyone had been in favor of a new courthouse instead of rebuilding the old one. The arguments over the two options faded and attention turned to naming a building commission and planning the new building.

Common Pleas Judge John P. Bailey was to name four members to a building commission to assist the Commissioners in the construction of the new courthouse. The Commission was urged to visit other counties who had built courthouses in the past ten years, to examine the materials, construction, and architecture, as new courthouses were being built with 'fire proof vaults and indoor plumbing'. The Sentinel article suggested that the contract for the architect be 'horse high, bull strong, and pig tight,' in order to avoid corruption and cost overruns. They urged that 'only honest and experienced men should be employed for this work, and that Putnam County can't afford to run a kindergarten school for the purpose of training inexperienced architects.'

Discussion was had about where the new building should be placed, and that the danger of high water should be considered. The old courthouse had been surrounded by water during past flooding and all now agreed that a basement would have resulted in greater damage. The square opposite the Public High School building on East Main was considered as an option to avoid flooding. The issue of tearing down the old courthouse before the new one was ready for occupancy was also discussed, but tearing down the old courthouse prior to construction would result in increased temporary office rental costs. The other consideration was the proximity of the Third Street jail near the existing Courthouse square, the jail having been completed some ten years earlier.

Requests were submitted for the appointment of a building commission and suggestions were made to appoint ex-prosecuting attorney B.A. Unverferth. Judge Bailey stated that the only demand he would make of the men appointed to the courthouse building commission was that they not spend any more than the amount appropriated by the voters.

By mid-October Judge Bailey made the appointment of four commissioners for courthouse construction. The men appointed were Dr. Warren R. Reed, Julius S. Ogan, Joseph C. Wannemacher, and Peter B. Hilty and they joined Commissioners Bernard A. Ruhe, Jacob Bright, and Jacob Best. Existing law provided for a balance of Republican and Democrat appointees.

In the weeks that followed the newspapers began to publish photos and descriptions of recently built Ohio courthouses. Design and costs were discussed and by early December applicants for an architect were reviewed by the building commission. The meetings of the commission had been in secret to this point, but discussion arose about whether to open them up to the public. The selection of an architect and the appointment of a superintendent of the upcoming work included references to construction problems in other counties and rumors of graft and corruption in secret deals of courthouse construction. The newspapers admonished the commission about possible bribes in the construction project.

An architectural contract was entered into with architect Frank L. Packard of Columbus in December of 1909, with the architect to be paid with a 5% building commission. Packard was an experienced architect who ultimately designed more than three thousand public buildings including three other Ohio courthouses and significant parts of Ohio State University, including the oval and surrounding buildings. He stated that he was considering the heating of the new building from the nearby electric light plant on Second Street, an 'effective and economical way to heat the building'. The architect stated that most large public buildings were being heated from a central heating plant, with steam or hot water pumped through underground pipes.

HON. JACOB BEST, COMMISSIONER.   HON. JACOB BRIGHT, COMMISSIONER.   HON. B. A. RUHE, COMMISSIONER.

HON. P. B. HILTY, PANDORA.

JUDGE JULIUS S. OGAN, OTTAWA.

DR. W. F. REED, OTTAWA.

HON. J. O. WANNEMACHER, OTTOVILLE.

IV Controversy

Putnam County citizens followed the debate over planning and construction of the courthouse through one of twelve county newspapers. The Putnam County Sentinel had moved to Ottawa in 1865 with the move of the county seat and claimed to have the largest circulation of the County. The paper was published on Fridays and was a vocal supporter of building the new courthouse. The rival Ottawa Gazette also published on Fridays and the offices were located across from the courthouse in the Odd Fellows block. The only German language newspaper of Putnam County was Der Demokrat, and was considered a must read for the many German speaking households in the county. Notices and information about the construction of the courthouse were published in the County newspapers on a weekly basis. Political controversies were debated in the papers concerning courthouse construction issues, costs, and the personalities of those involved in the building committee and construction.

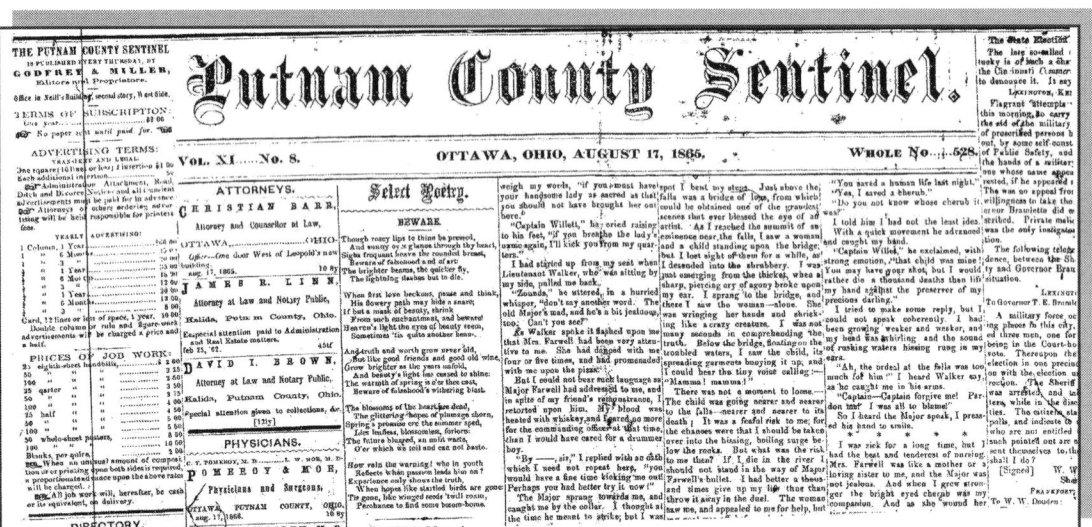

Controversy over Judge Bailey's appointments to the Building Commission was the front-page headline news of June 1st, 1910. Democratic and Republican statements about the Sentinel's role in the appointment of the Commission were argued about between the Ottawa Gazette and the Sentinel, one paper supporting the Democratic Party and one supporting the Republican Party.

The newspaper in letters and editorials accused the opposing paper of misstatements concerning where the courthouse would be placed and about the process for the appointment

of the Commission. The Sentinel was accused of manipulating Judge Bailey and of encouraging that the old courthouse be torn down immediately. Newspaper bickering included accusations that 'the German citizens of the county were being insulted' by personal statements made by an anonymous individual concerning the process.

Construction work began on June 24, 1910 and proceeded on schedule. Construction was to be completed within one year. An order issued by the Commission instructed that an inspector be present at all times, ensuring that 'cement was properly mixed, and that taxpayers would not be fooled'.

By August of 1909, a resolution was introduced by Commissioner Jacob Best requesting that the newspapers publish all the proceedings and minutes of the Building Commission, in order to give taxpayers information about construction. The resolution was defeated in a five to two vote. The resolution was reintroduced before the County Commissioners, that 'the taxpayers are desirous of knowing what the Courthouse Building Commission has done and are doing and the County auditor is to furnish a copy of all proceedings had by the Commission to the twelve County newspapers requesting them'. The resolution was passed on a two to one vote.

VI. Plans to begin Construction

By March of 1910 a courthouse fire destroyed the Adams County Courthouse. Most of the records were destroyed and the cost of replacing the records was thought to be considerable. The Sentinel reminded the County that the safety of official records should be a first concern and that the county should be on guard day and night until county records are safely stored in the new fireproof vaults at the new courthouse.

By April 1910 anxious citizens were asking when the construction of the courthouse would begin. Described as the biggest undertaking in the county's history, citizens were anxious to break ground. The money provisions had been settled and the architectural design had been agreed upon, details were being processed.

A dispute continued as to whether the new Courthouse should be built in the center of the existing lot or whether the old Courthouse should be torn down before the construction began.

Changes in infrastructure were discussed, including the laying of the steam line from the Village power plant on Second Street for heating the new building. New telephone poles and lines were reconfigured for the Courthouse and waterworks trustees were to reset one of the water mains to the center of the Courthouse grounds. The question remained whether the Village or the County would pay for the electric light plant expenses for the county plan to put in a central heating system and heat the courthouse and jail with the steam line. A franchise was granted to lay pipes along East Main Street, although the Village council was reluctant to grant the request which would require tearing up the pavement. The contract for the steam line remained controversial and in litigation for many years and, as with numerous other statewide public projects, was abandoned as unworkable within a few years.

Elections were approaching for the County Commissioners. The Democrats had a two terms only policy for Commissioner and it was 'doubtful that the Democratic committee would think of endorsing any existing person for another term'. Multiple terms were condemned by both parties.

By mid-April 1910 the Courthouse Commission was divided on the location of the new building. The original plan provided for construction in part on the lot where the old courthouse stood, which would require tearing down the North end of the old courthouse to allow for construction. Judge Bailey advised that the back portion of the old courthouse could not be safely removed, and that the rest of the building would be usable. The commissioners considered moving the building farther north in the lot, in part to avoid the building 'being too near the back door of a foul smelling horse stable'. The Building Commission finally decided to build directly behind the existing courthouse near the center of the lot. After the location was decided, the commission adopted the architect's plan by unanimous vote.

Sentiment about the old courthouse continued to be part of the planning. A farmer proposed that some of the bricks of the old courthouse be used to build an assembly hall at the Fairgrounds, in order to preserve part of the building for future generations. The Sentinel noted that the old courthouse had been the scene of many 'interesting trials in which human lives were the stakes'. The paper reminisced about jury decisions and criminals sentenced at court, with a broken hearted wife or mother. The paper noted that a past judge had pronounced the sentence of death in the courthouse and good men as jurors had contended with their convictions in determining verdicts as to who was right and who was wrong. Life events such as marriages and divorces had occurred at the old courthouse and the paper noted that the building is 'not simply a pile of brick, and stone, and mortar, but rather is history, memories, gladness, sadness, smiles, tears, heartaches, regrets and all the other moments of human life'.

On Saturday May 18, 1910, the sealed bids for new a courthouse were opened before a large crowd by the Courthouse Commission. The Architect oversaw the opening of ten bids for the entire project. Bids were broken down by work to be performed and materials; overall periods were entered in amounts from $177,000 $204,000. The low bid was Evans and Company at $177,931. The Commission began the process of determining whether to award the bid to one general contractor or consider breaking down the several contracts in an attempt to reduce the cost. A skeptical newspaper challenged that the Commission should determine whether there was a conspiracy to let certain subcontractors receive a contract at the expense of the taxpayers.

Total bids were as follows

---

136 Commissioners' Journal, Putnam Co., Session, MAY 1909 A. D. 190

proposition and not taking into consideration the alternates, was $180,613.19.

A schedule of the ten complete bids is given below, from which the difference in the amount of the various bids may be readily observed:

Comparison No. 1

R.H. Evans & Company,	Zanesville, O.	$177931.00
George A. Abernethy	Columbus, O.	180500.00
Karg & Steinle,--Westerville and Fremont, O.		183450.00
George Feick	Sandusky, O.	184268.00
W.W. Luyster	Dayton, O.	190350.00
National Concrete Fireproofing Co.	Cleveland, O.	191200.00
Nichol and Carr	Columbus, O.	193700.00
The Francis Brothers Company	Columbus, O.	197720.00
Henry Shenk Company	Erie, Pa.	204494.00
Henry L. Van der Horst	Kalamazoo, Mich.	209627.00

On the straight proposition, for the work complete, it will be observed that R.H. Evans & Company are the lowest bidders and Mr. Abernethy the second lowest bidder.

Taking into consideration certain of the alternate propositions as hereinafter explained, we beg to make a comparison of the four lowest bids, these being the bids of R.H. Evans & Company, Mr. George A. Abernethy, Karg & Steinle and Mr. George

VII. Construction Moves Forward

Construction continued in January of 1911 on the outside steel and stone structure of the building. The old Courthouse remained standing and continued to house the offices for the County.

On January 6, 1911 at about three in the morning a fire broke out at a blacksmith shop located on Second Street, a block from the courthouse. One of the firemen responding to the fire was the courthouse janitor Joseph Hermiller, well known to many in the county. Hermiller and another volunteer were electrocuted by fallen electrical wires; several other volunteers were injured trying to assist them. A memorial service at the Presbyterian Church next to the courthouse construction was attended by county officials and fire departments from surrounding towns.

By February of 1911, the Courthouse was described as 'imposing in appearance and was set to be one of the models of the future in the state'. Articles noted that 'skilled workmen carried and placed stone in all kinds of weather to complete the contract within the specified time'. It was stated that 'Architect Packard will make good on his claim of one of the finest courthouses in the state'. Significant progress was noted in the first week of February and the newspaper reported that the taxpayers are getting a good benefit for their tax dollar.

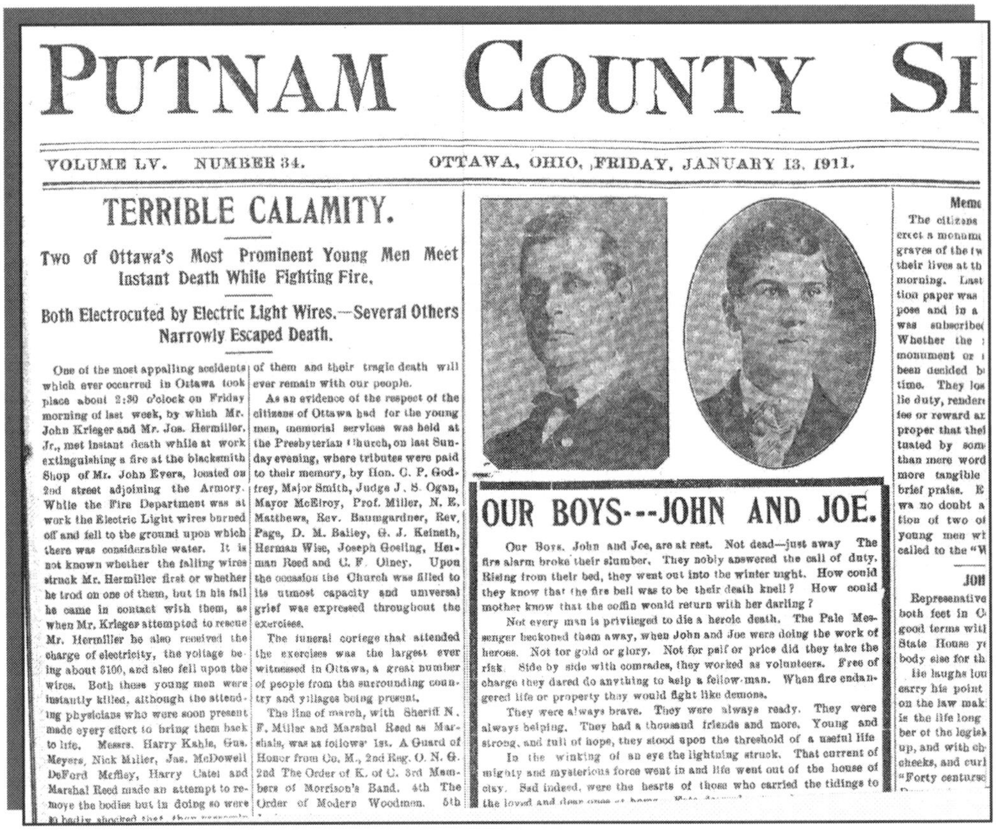

PUTNAM COUNTY SI

VOLUME LV. NUMBER 34. OTTAWA, OHIO, FRIDAY, JANUARY 13, 1911.

TERRIBLE CALAMITY.

Two of Ottawa's Most Prominent Young Men Meet Instant Death While Fighting Fire.

Both Electrocuted by Electric Light Wires.—Several Others Narrowly Escaped Death.

One of the most appalling accidents which ever occurred in Ottawa took place about 2:30 o'clock on Friday morning of last week, by which Mr. John Krieger and Mr. Jos. Hermiller, Jr., met instant death while at work extinguishing a fire at the blacksmith Shop of Mr. John Evers, located on 2nd street adjoining the Armory. While the Fire Department was at work the Electric Light wires burned off and fell to the ground upon which there was considerable water. It is not known whether the falling wires struck Mr. Hermiller first or whether he trod on one of them, but in his fall he came in contact with them, as when Mr. Krieger attempted to rescue Mr. Hermiller he also received the charge of electricity, the voltage being about 2100, and also fell upon the wires. Both these young men were instantly killed, although the attending physicians who were soon present made every effort to bring them back to life. Messrs. Harry Kahle, Gus. Meyers, Nick Miller, Jas. McDowell DeFord Meffley, Harry Uatel and Marshal Reed made an attempt to remove the bodies but in doing so were so badly shocked that they ...

... of them and their tragic death will ever remain with our people.

As an evidence of the respect of the citizens of Ottawa had for the young men, memorial services was held at the Presbyterian Church, on last Sunday evening, where tributes were paid to their memory, by Hon. C. P. Godfrey, Major Smith, Judge J. S. Ogan, Mayor McElroy, Prof. Miller, N. E. Matthews, Rev. Baumgardner, Rev. Page, D. M. Bailey, G. J. Keineth, Herman Wise, Joseph Gosling, Herman Reed and C. F. Olney. Upon the occasion the Church was filled to its utmost capacity and universal grief was expressed throughout the exercises.

The funeral cortege that attended the exercises was the largest ever witnessed in Ottawa, a great number of people from the surrounding country and villages being present.

The line of march, with Sheriff N. F. Miller and Marshal Reed as Marshals, was as follows: 1st. A Guard of Honor from Co. M., 2nd Reg. O. N. G. 2nd The Order of K. of C. 3rd Members of Morrison's Band. 4th The Order of Modern Woodmen. 5th ...

OUR BOYS---JOHN AND JOE.

Our Boys, John and Joe, are at rest. Not dead—just away The fire alarm broke their slumber. They nobly answered the call of duty. Rising from their bed, they went out into the winter night. How could they know that the fire bell was to be their death knell? How could mother know that the coffin would return with her darling?

Not every man is privileged to die a heroic death. The Pale Messenger beckoned them away, when John and Joe were doing the work of heroes. Not for gold or glory. Not for pelf or price did they take the risk. Side by side with comrades, they worked as volunteers. Free of charge they dared do anything to help a fellow-man. When fire endangered life or property they would fight like demons.

They were always brave. They were always ready. They were always helping. They had a thousand friends and more. Young and strong, and full of hope, they stood upon the threshold of a useful life.

In the winking of an eye the lightning struck. That current of mighty and mysterious force went in and life went out of the house of clay. Sad indeed, were the hearts of those who carried the tidings to the loved and dear ones at home. ...

Memo...

The citizens ... erect a monum... graves of the tw... their lives at th... morning. Last ... tion paper was ... pose and in a ... was subscribed ... Whether the ... monument or ... been decided b... time. They los... lic duty, render... fee or reward a... proper that the... tuated by som... than mere word... more tangible ... brief praise. ... wa no doubt a... tion of two of ... young men wh... called to the "W...

JOH...

Representative ... both feet in C... good terms with ... State House y... body else for th...

He laughs lou... carry his point ... on the law mak... is the life long ... ber of the legisl... up, and with ch... cheeks, and curl... "Forty centurse...

Attention turned to the furniture and fixtures inside of the building. The building commission was to issue orders for fixtures and furniture throughout the new building and was urged to use their best business judgment to avoid the scandal in connection with other public construction projects. The new building was to be 'the finest in Ohio with the furniture and fixtures to be first-class and in keeping with the splendid appearance of the new structure'.

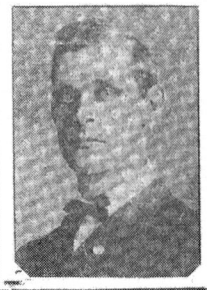

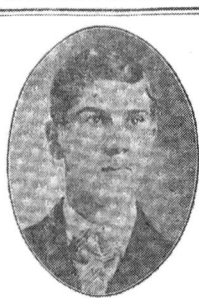

During the construction phase another controversy with county officials continued. A state examiner had made findings that monies were improperly paid to several county officials through improper draws for payment. However, this did not directly affect courthouse construction. The Sentinel strongly defended the actions of county officials and questioned the motives of the state examiner who was making the accusations.

VIII. Construction Nears Completion

Significant progress was made on the new Courthouse by June of 1911, and the building was described as 'majestic and imposing'. The newspapers continued to note that the taxpayers had fared well and that 'no graft had tainted the construction'. Architect Packard was praised for 'bringing forth extraordinary effort to make it one of the best monuments of his skill as a builder'. The newspaper noted that the building should 'endure for 100 years or more and the foundation stones rest on soil that is good'.

The question of decorating the interior continued to be an issue for the Building Commission. Local sentiment held that the 'work of decorating the interior should be under the direction of N P Schumacher, formerly of Riley Township, now living in Chicago, with a splendid reputation as a skillful decorator and designer'. He had completed several large contacts previously and had performed well. The paper urged that this local boy be given an opportunity. The papers did not later report that Schumacher was given the job.

By the end of 1911 the new courthouse was nearing completion. The December tax payment was to be the 'last time the taxpayers would pay taxes in the old building and it was anticipated that Judge Bailey had started the last court record under the old roof'. The upcoming dedication of the new building was considered to be one of the biggest historical events of the County. The newspaper suggested that Governor Harman, described as the next president, should be invited to attend as well as the Judges of the Supreme Court and Circuit Courts. It was also suggested that United States Senators should be invited and that County officials of other adjacent counties should also be invited to attend. They also suggested that schools, churches, farmers, businessmen, as well as fraternal organization should be officially represented and that mayors and other county officials should attend.

The question next became whether a dedication should occur before or after the old building was torn down and the rubbish cleared away. The Building Commission was to make this decision. The paper observed that the taxpayers would not have any regrets when they were invited to visit the county seat and inspect the newly completed building. The honest and faithful service of the building commission was noted, including that on 'dedication day that the taxpayers would appreciate the value received'. The paper noted that in 50 years that school children of today would be proud to say that they were present at the Courthouse dedication and that as many schoolchildren as possible should attend this historic event and that front seats should be given to those with anything to do with the building of the Courthouse. The paper urged that 'farm boys should ride to Ottawa on horseback and the girl should ride in gaily decorated wagons and that this would not be too much fuss and feathers. The building should be dedicated in the name of God, morality, justice, progress, and good citizenship in public service. It will endure for centuries'.

The Courthouse was accepted by the County Commissioners from the architect and contractor on May 21, 1912. No record has been found of any formal dedication of the building.

IX. CORRELATION TO THE NARRATIVE

01. Preliminary Study and Sketches

President of the Building Commission Bernard A. Ruhe called a meeting for December 9, 1909. At that time the commission ordered a preliminary study and sketches to be completed by architect Packard for a building with a ground floor, first floor, and second floor. The first view and description of the soon-to-be built courthouse was published in the *Putnam County Sentinel* on January 21, 1910, with a detailed description from the architect. The proposed new courthouse was described as follows. The article is condensed.

∧∧∧∧∧∧∧∧∧∧

The ground floor, which will be about three feet above the sidewalk level, embraces a reception room which is provided with a check room and toilets. This will be open and accessible to anyone of the county or to visitors where they check their wraps or packages or avail themselves of the toilet privileges. This floor [first] will have separate rooms for the coroner, infirmary directors, board of elections, board of school examiners, and a Grand Army of the Republic [G.A.R.] room for use by the G.A.R. or other societies as well as a relic room and museum. An office was provided for the building custodian and an assembly hall to accommodate about three hundred people.

There are three principle entrances to the ground floor, one each on Main Street, Third Street, and Hickory Street. There will also be an entrance from the alley [west] side. The second floor is accessible from the ground floor by a spacious stairway or by an elevator.

On the second floor will be located the recorder's rooms, consisting of a public room, abstract room and record room, and the treasurer's office with public room, record room and vault. Connected with the treasurer's office is the auditor's office with public room, work room, and record room. Connected with the auditor's office are the county commissioners' quarters with public room and work room. Next to the commissioners' office is the office of the surveyor [county engineer] with public room and work room in connection.

At the end of the public lobby, opposite the treasurer's office, is the office for the probate judge with record room and court room in connection. This court room is large enough to accommodate the circuit court should it be necessary to use it for that purpose. The general lavatories for men will be located on this floor while the lavatories for women are located on the ground floor.

On the third floor is the common pleas court room which is amply large. Opening off of this court room is a judge's room with private room in connection. In close connection with this court room is a room for male witnesses and the stenographer's room. The [county] clerk's room with public room and record room is located on this floor. Closely connected are the rooms for the sheriff, petit jury, prosecuting attorney and a consultation room with private lavatory.

At the south end of the public lobby, opposite the common pleas court, is the grand jury room. Another judge's room is provided near the grand jury room and also a law library, ante room, female witness room, and women's retiring room and lavatories.

The public lobbies and corridors are spacious and well lighted. All rooms are easily accessible from the corridors. All sharp angles and other objectionable features have been eliminated from the plan.

∧∧∧∧∧∧∧∧∧∧

An artist's rendition of the exterior of the building itself showed full-sized stylized lions reclining on either side of the entrance steps near the doors. These were never placed. Instead a lion's head was placed on each side of the door at the top of columns which appear to be supporting "the centrally-positioned front and rear entrances that are covered by small stone balconies with stone balustrades."

The use of the ground floor toilets that were to be "open and accessible" even when the courthouse was not officially open, continued to be a topic of discussion in the years that followed construction. A front page article in the *Sentinel* dated April 7, 1922 was titled *A Public Convenience.* It stated that at the last meeting of the Chamber of Commerce one of the members noted that the public was very much inconvenienced on Saturdays and Sundays by not having a downtown public toilet available. The Chamber members suggested that the county commissioners be approached about having the lobby of the courthouse open for such purpose. The Chamber board of directors approved this suggestion but pointed out that children and careless adults had littered the restroom floors in the past requiring that the courthouse lobby be closed to prevent damage to the building.

The Chamber committee later reported that the commissioners were courteous and willing to grant the privilege and accordingly opened the lobby until 11:00 PM on Wednesdays and Saturdays and all day on Sunday. The commissioners pointed out that "rowdyism" would not be tolerated and that the privilege should not be abused. Thereafter citizens recalled having the restroom facilities available as they attended a movie in one of the downtown Ottawa theaters or shopped in downtown stores.

02. Elected Officials

In 2013 the configuration of the courthouse rooms remains much the same as the way they were planned 100 years ago but some occupancy has changed.

Offices: on the first floor Commissioners John E. Love, Vincent T. Schroeder, and Travis A. Jerwers; on the second floor Probate/Juvenile Judge Michael A. Borer, Engineer Terrence R. Recker, Auditor Robert L. Benroth, Treasurer Tracy L. Warnecke, and Recorder Cathy S. Recker; on the third floor Common Pleas Judge Randall L. Basinger, County Municipal Court Judge Chad C. Niese, and Clerk of Courts Teresa J. Lammers. Coroner Anna M. Horstman has her office at her medical practice in Kalida, Prosecuting Attorney Gary L. Lammers has his office in the County Annex Building on East Main Street, and Sheriff Michael C. Chandler is in his office at the county jail building on Heritage Trail in Ottawa.

Photos of past Common Pleas Judges line the walls of the main court room on the third floor. The first judges of the court were appointed in 1834 and charged with the responsibility of officially organizing Putnam County. Other elected officials have plaques in their offices that list all of their predecessors from 1834 forward.

03. 'Putnam County Courthouse Built'

Photographs of the 'Putnam County Courthouse, built 1909-1913' were published in the *Architectural Review* magazine in 1914. The magazine is a monthly international architectural publication printed in London since 1896 and dedicated to architectural and building issues. The 1914 photo of the third floor corridor shows little change from 2013. The clock has been replaced with a larger wooden clock and the brass spittoon no longer sits in the hallway. The walls show the rusticated courses of stone which at one time were to be marble. The original bench remains in 2013. The wooden hallway chair shown in the photo has been moved to become the alternate juror's seat in the main courtroom.

04. Second Floor Corridor

The 1914 photo of the second-floor corridor shows a light fixture similar to ones still in use on the third floor. Spittoon's were purchased for $86 and used throughout the building. The elevator originally built in the courthouse was operated by a courthouse employee and was referred to by some as an 'up-and-down wagon' and that some farmers remarked that going up was fine but that going down caused you to feel that you should have walked down the stairs.

05. Interior of Principal Courtroom

The original photo of the interior of the principal courtroom shows the witness box on the opposite side of where it currently exists in 2013. The remaining furnishings and light fixtures of the room are all original. The room was repainted in 1995 using original colors. The walls of the main courtroom are now covered with tile for help with acoustics, but were originally built with courses of Caen stone, made to look rusticated or old as now remains in the hallways. Caen stone is a type of easily cut creamy yellow limestone originally used in Caen, France for building projects in the Roman period and later in the middle ages. The room was completed with a pattern of twelve, designed to represent twelve jurors and includes lighting fixtures with twelve lights, twelve sets of pillars, twelve skylights in any section, and twelve benches for observers.

06. Extensive Marble

   Extensive marble was used throughout the building. Plans for marble in the interior hallways was changed by the building commission, resulting in a savings of $8,000. This savings would represent nearly a $1 million savings in 2013 money. The placement of marble included specific direction by the architect as to the type of marble and the pattern to be used. Floors throughout the building including the hallways, some office entrances, and restrooms were to be Vermont marble in colors shown on the drawings. The marble was to be free from any stain and in patterns shown. The main corridors were to have a variance of no more than one fourth of an inch in a run of fifty feet, the Architect stating that 'nothing but a perfect job of marble floor work would be accepted'. The marble was milled off-site according to the specification, crated, and then shipped by train to be reconstructed on the site. The main stairway from the ground-floor to the third floor was built on a concrete base over a steel frame and then covered with marble casing. The balustrade, handrail, and endposts of the main staircase are light cloud Vermont marble and were sand rubbed and polished according to the specifications. The corridors are quality selected Hauteville marble.. The private and public washrooms included marble wainscot and floors with brass fittings, and were to be first quality white Italian stock marble with all the veining to match.

07. Construction Continued

Construction continued through 1910 with workers from R. H. Evans Construction Company. The architect and construction superintendent worked out of a separate construction office with a telephone built on site to provide access to blueprints. A temporary water closet was constructed for workers. A temporary flight of rough stairs with hand rails was built from the ground floor to the attic for use by workers. Strict rules required that any contractor be responsible for his own materials and that red lights be placed upon all obstructions at night. Safety rules were in place to prevent accidents, and a solid ten foot high board fence entirely enclosing the building denied access to the public.

Concrete used in the building was composed of one part cement, two and one half parts sand and four parts broken stone and was machine mixed on-site. Specifications included that the very best quality clean sharp Canadian Lake Sand be used and that it was to be inspected and tested in accordance with the specifications.

The limestone walls called for a commercial graded Royal Blue Bedford limestone cut to exact specifications, with blocks of limestone cut to be interchangeable from one section of the building to another. Specifications required that all the stone come from an operating quarry to ensure a ready supply and that the supplier be able to show examples of the stone from the quarry in other buildings built in the previous ten years. All stone was sawed and chiseled and sand rubbed to a smooth uniform surface in a most careful and workmanlike manner and in strict accordance with the drawings. Ornamental limestone in friezes and decorations on the outside of the building were carved by skilled subcontractors and shipped to Ottawa.

Steel used in construction was to be forged in the latest technology on an open hearth or Bessemer process. The entrance vestibule walls are Buff Amherst sandstone.

08. Ornamental Wall and Ceiling Plaster

Ornamental wall and ceiling plastering was shown in detail on scale drawings. The plaster work is composed of one part seasoned paste, one part clean lake sand, with sufficient quantity of cow's hair to ensure a good bond. Wooden moulds were carved to specifications and approved by the architect before the plastering was cast in strict accordance with details and approved by the architect.

09. Lumber and Interior Finish

All lumber for interior finish was to be selected first quality quarter sawed white oak; flooring was 7/8 inch quarter sawed oak. Quarter sawing is done by cutting the log into quarters before boards are cut, resulting in narrower boards with distinctive grain lines. The technique was more expensive and was sometimes used in furniture making and finely detailed work. Other three dimensional wood carving in the court rooms were hand carved from whole pieces of oak.

10. Skylights and Stained Glass

The skylights were made of hard copper and glazed with wire woven glass, built at the proper angle to deflect light onto the ceiling panels below.

The art stained glass was to be done in a careful and workmanlike manner and was contracted separately by the building commission at a cost of $1500 (approximately $150,000 in 2013 equivalent). Patriotic and repeated themes such as cherubs appear in the glass panels dated 1911.

Six paintings line the top of the central staircase

11. Flood of 1913

The flood of 1913 occurred within two months after all of the county elected officials had moved into their offices in the brand-new courthouse. The town was swept by water 33.30 feet deep, and highest in the history of the Village of Ottawa to date, 2013.

"Out of the darkness of Monday night, March 24, 1913 came the rushing, raging flood. Swift and sure it went high, then higher, then highest in the history of the town. ... All railways were paralyzed. Boats were lacking. Travel at a standstill. But lightening flashed a message over the wires and soon men, boats, food, and help were on the way. From Leipsic, Columbus Grove, Lima, Toledo, St. Marys and other places relief came at double quick. Farmers came with wagon loads of supplies of food and fuel. This kindly action was of their own motion. They did not wait to be asked to help. ..." *Putnam County Sentinel,* March 28, 1913

Court House history comes to life through memories

*Teresa Lammers and Susan Basinger interviewed s
several people about their memories of the court house*

Wisdom From the Past:

A news article outlining the history of the Putnam County Courthouse, written by Judge Randall Basinger, was printed in a Toledo Magazine in 1988. Within a few weeks of the stories' appearance in print Judge Basinger received a letter from R. L. Roose of Maumee who told Judge Basinger that he had enjoyed reading the story about the Putnam County Courthouse. He then went on to say, "My disagreement with your date of 1912 is offered in only the mildest and friendly protest."

Mr. Roose stated in his letter that exception might be taken to the memory of a 16-year-old boy who was writing the letter 76 years after its occurrence. He went on to explain in his letter that his family moved to Ottawa in the autumn of 1911 and his father, John E. Roose, was the first auditor to serve in the new building. The name, John E. Roose, appears on the plaque in the front hall of the courthouse today.

Mr. Roose stated in his letter, *"I worked for my father as a clerk part of 1915 and 1916 and went to Ohio State University in autumn 1917. The newness of the offices and the clear, clean marble so much used throughout the building are in my lasting memory."* Other memories shared by Mr. Roose included:

"Of course, people came on business from all parts of the county. One day, I dashed in the "Mens" room and embarrassed a man who, never having seen an indoor flush toilet said, 'I guess I am in the wrong place'. He had his suspenders and pants down and trying to climb up onto a wash basin. I directed him through the swinging door and that day a Putnam County resident learned the comfort of an indoor flush toilet".

"I worked near a front window, second floor. One day a happened to see a very beautiful young lady throwing a kiss in my direction. Thrilling, of course, until I remembered her hostess cousin who worked in the office above me".

"Mr. Barney Kroeger was the janitor, as called in those days. His step ladder (called up, or oop ladder by him) had been borrowed and returned. He was asked the meaning of the letters BKK painted on the ladder and he replied, 'Barney Kroeger Korthouse'."

"The building was first heated by exhaust steam piped from the Ottawa owned light plant. Later coal was used. Perhaps cleaner gas is used now. In 1920 I left Ottawa, returning only for short visits. In 1958 I had the occasion to enter the building. I was sad to see the black coal and other dirt of nearly forty years. If the county ever paid the high cost for restoring the building to its original beauty inside and outside. I would make every effort to get to see it again even having had 92 birthdays."

There has been much activity around the Putnam County Courthouse of 2013 in preparation of its 100th birthday. Along with customary daily work, extra efforts of refurbishing, painting, washing and scrubbing has occurred. Please take the advise of Mr. M. L. Roose and visit this beautiful monument which has witnessed 100 years of growth and change in Putnam County.

"That's just what they did back then."

Jane Hermiller was born in 1921 and grew up with her family south of Ottawa. Her husband, Francis, who is also 91 years of age, was a "town kid". On July 10th this year they celebrated their 65th wedding anniversary. Their memories of the Putnam County Courthouse add to the treasury of purposes the building has witnessed over the past 100 years.

Jane has a unique memory dating back to 1928 when she had her tonsils and adenoids taken out at the age of seven. "There were seven of us in the clinic that day in the Courthouse. My family doctor, Dr. Piatt, did the procedure," Jane recalled. "I went home a little while after it was completed. I don't remember feeling real bad or anything," she added. She and Francis thought those clinics occurred into the mid 1930's.

Francis was the oldest of five children and recalls his mother coming to the courthouse to receive 'relief' supplies after his father died when he was eleven years old in 1933. "Mom would pull a little red wagon to the west door of the courthouse to pick up the basic food supplies that were offered," Francis remembered and added "I believe that occurred once a month or so".

Francis is also known as Hank. "I answer to both names," Hank said with a chuckle. He began working at the Kroger Grocery Store located across Main Street from the Courthouse when he was in High School and worked there until he was drafted in 1942. "I was paid $13 per week for my work and I thought it was a pretty good job", he remembered. "Saturday night was the time when many people came to town with their family to shop, visit and go to the taverns and movie theaters. The store would stay open until people went home for the evening after all their activities. They would purchase their groceries and we would keep them in the store until they were ready to go home. I didn't like how late we stayed open sometimes," Hank recalled. He also remembered that the Kroger Store carried Spotlight coffee and the A & P Grocery located on the nearby corner carried 8 O'Clock coffee. "It was a time before grocery carts and we would fill customer orders for them," he stated. "I remember those two brands of coffee".

The Hermillers remembered how important and what an essential part of life those Saturday nights in Ottawa were for families. Everyone could find something to do regardless of their age. They recalled that the public library was located in the Courthouse and the building would be open for people to visit.

Hank recalled Mrs. Evelyn Blossom, from the Draft Board when he registered for military service and when he reported for duty during World War II. He also stated that Army personnel stressed that they have their discharge papers recorded in the Courthouse when they were released from service at the Soldiers and Sailors Relief office.

The couple recalled applying for their marriage license 65 years ago with Rose Mary Furrogh, an employee of Judge J. Harry Leopold, at a time when blood tests were required to obtain the license.

The parents of four children, the Hermiller's visited the Courthouse for the customary reasons dictated by a growing family. "I do remember being called for jury duty a couple of times through the years," Hank stated "But don't remember exactly what they were about." Jane remembered involvement in a case when she witnessed an accident.

We may view their unique memories of the Courthouse as something very much out of the ordinary for 2013 standards, they both only remarked, "That's just what they did back then".

"I remembered thinking those windows were really something!"

William (Bill) Schroeder is 96 years old and has lived his entire life on the family homestead at 13785 Road H-13, northwest of Ottawa. His birth date is March 5, 1917, and the newly constructed Putnam County Courthouse was in it's fourth year of use when he was born. Bill's earliest memory of the Courthouse was traveling by horse and wagon to Ottawa. One of the stops would be the Courthouse to register their dog. "We always walked in from the south side of town and I'm sure there was a place to keep the horses but I can't quite remember where that would have been", Bill said. He recalled with a chuckle that the workers would ask for a description of his dog, what kind, spots and marks, and it would be a dollar for the license and metal tags. Some still hang in his buildings on the farm.

"I remember thinking those windows were really something, all those colors", Bill described the stained glass windows which light the open stairway between the first and second floors. "I really liked those big swinging doors into the building. Most kids wouldn't see that kind of thing very often, Bill recalled and added "Mom and I would take the elevator but Dad always took the steps. We heard stories about people getting stuck in that elevator and they could be in there a half day until they got them out".

As Bill grew he remembered traveling to the Courthouse with his Dad to take care of legal issues upon purchase of an 80-acre farm in the Leipsic area which he thought cost about $7,000.00. "Those were the days that you could get a lawyer to do some things for you and they would charge you a few dollars. Not that way today," Bill reminisced. Another stop at the Courthouse would be the Treasurer's office to pay taxes according to Bill. "That office would provide extra cash also so you wouldn't have to make another stop" he remembered and then added "You had to be careful when going to the Courthouse especially during the depression. Many people needed help and if they thought you had money on you they might try something."

Another memory Bill had of going to the Courthouse was the Draft Board to register for military services. "I was sent notice to report to the draft board three times" Bill recalled, "One time they took a couple of bus loads of guys to Columbus for tests. But I never was called to serve in World War II".

"He was so happy and proud to have that piece of paper"

Reminiscing about trips to the Putnam County Courthouse brought many lifetime experiences to the forefront and laughter for a group of residents at the Putnam Acres Care Center (Meadows) located east of Ottawa on Road 5-H. When asked about memories of the Putnam County Courthouse while growing up, familiar purposes to visit the county seat were to pay taxes, purchasing dog tags, vaccinations and marriage licenses.

Agnes Rice was born in Russia and came to the United States with her family when she was 9 years old. Her family settled in the Pandora community. She recalled going to the Courthouse almost 75 years ago when she was 17 years old to purchase her marriage license with her soon-to-be husband, Melvin. She said she knew she might have a problem since she was not yet 18 years old and needed the consent of her parents. Their trip was not in vain however, as the probate juvenile court judge at that time, Judge George, knew her and allowed the license to be issued. "Melvin's father, who cut wood for a living provided wood for heating the Courthouse and was acquainted with the Judge," Agnes recalled.

Agnes talked about her experience with jury duty over 30 years ago. "The man on trial was a black man who got himself into trouble at the county fair," she recalled. She remembered being questioned about her opinion concerning African American people. One of the questions was "How do you relate to negroes," she said. I answered that I never had to mingle with them so I had no opinion. "I was dismissed from jury duty but I don't know why," Agnes concluded her story.

Agnes also remembered times when the side doors of the courthouse were locked and the public had to use the front door for entrance but did not remember why that was done. She also recalled that the restrooms were either not available to the public or were not in the Courthouse in the early years. She told with a chuckle that the driver's license exams were given at the Courthouse years ago. "I thought I knew it all on my first attempt at taking the test and I flunked," she said. "But I did not flunk the second time".

Agnes was not the only member of the group to be called for jury duty. Mae Wells, an Ottoville resident, remembered reporting at the Courthouse for jury duty and hearing a case concerning a man who had caused damage to another person's vehicle in a accident with a trailer. She was not sure about the details of that service but recalled a time when her brother-in-law was called for jury duty. "When told a few specifics of the case he told the attorney 'He's guilty' and he did not have to serve," Agnes said, "I guess that was one way to do it".

Mae proudly told of one of her boys recently showing her a darkened piece of old paper which was the original discharge military document for her husband, Bud, who had served in World War II. He acquired the document from the Veteran's Service office at the Courthouse. "He is interested in family history and wanted to write a story about his Dad," she said. "He was so happy and proud to have that piece of paper".   Mae lightheartedly shared with the group about how she married her husband who will turn 90 years old in July. The couple share a room at the Putnam Acres facility. Mae said her husband's first wife had died leaving him and their three sons. "I was 22 and he was 32 years old and I always told people that he needed a wife, the boys needed a mother and I didn't want to be an old maid," Mae chuckled and then added, "He got so aggravated and told me to stop saying that".

Sally Schmidt, who was born and raised in the Cloverdale area and later lived in Ottawa and Leipsic communities, shared how she once had to go to the Courthouse to pay a traffic fine. "I don't believe that stop light in Leipsic was working right and I went through and hit another vehicle," she recalled and then added, "I had to pay 60 dollars because of that light". Another participant in the discussion group was Sally's sister, Henrietta Wischmeyer, who also lives at Putnam Acres. Henrietta grew up in Cloverdale and moved to Glandorf after she was married.

Mary Ann Radabaugh, was born in Lima but has lived in Leipsic and Ottawa during her lifetime. She remembered being in the Courthouse for various legal reasons over the years especially when she applied for her marriage license 42 years ago. One of Mary Ann's unique stories was being subpoenaed as a witness in a court case after a young woman stole a Wii game from the Putnam Acres facility. "I watched her do it," Mary Ann recalled. "When it came time for the hearing they couldn't find her and I never had to go to court," she concluded.

Mary Ann shared various visits she made to the Courthouse concerning birth and adoption records. Her mother was born at home in July 21, 1919 and she told of their attempts to acquire a birth certificate for her. She also told of her search to find her birth mother which began at the Allen County Courthouse but was successful when they researched at the Putnam County Courthouse and found the birth record of her mother as well as the birth records of her grandparents and their marriage record. She also recalled her happy trip to the Courthouse when she adopted her children, Mary Sue at age 6 and Rick at age 7.

Memories of county men who served during war time surfaced as Mary Ann told of the clock which stands in front of the Courthouse dedicated to her uncle, Leo Kerner, who died while serving during World War I. Members of group shared memories of reading through the large plaques displayed on the first floor of the Courthouse listing the names of all county residents who served in military service. Many family names appear on the plaques including the son of Agnes Rice who served in the Vietnam War.

Other residents sharing in the group included Helen Schroeder who grew up in the Miller City community before her marriage took her to the Columbus Grove area. Shirley Miller was born and raised in Lima but also became a member of the Columbus Grove community during her adult life. Cora Nauveau came from Henry County to live in the Leipsic area.

Activity director, Theresa Meyer, recalled sitting on the hard hall benches while waiting her turn for vaccinations at the Health Department located in the Courthouse at one time. The group agreed that many of their families came to the Courthouse to receive the polio vaccine in the sugar cube 45 to 50 years ago. Other recollections of the group included the beautiful windows in the courthouse, especially the stained glass between the first and second floors.

It was agreed the Courthouse always looks beautiful when it is decorated during the Christmas holiday. Although other festive occasions could not be immediately recalled it was mentioned that the Courthouse seemed to be along the parade route during a variety of celebrations such as the annual county fair. Mary Ann Radabaugh remembered the fire trucks transporting the 1950 Miller City State Championship Basketball team down Main Street past the Courthouse when they returned from Columbus on their journey to their home town.

"I collected the Courthouse news and my employer printed the 'Scandal Sheet".

It is one's location in life that often determines exposure to the new. This became apparent when a group of residents of The Meadows Care facility in Kalida met to share memories of visits to Ottawa and the Putnam County Courthouse. For many, Wednesday and Saturday evenings often brought a trip to 'town' to purchase necessities and to socialize with friends and neighbors. Town was the nearest community in traveling distance, not necessarily the county seat of Ottawa. It was agreed that travel distance was the reason for the self sufficiency of most small villages located throughout Putnam County during the past 100 years and also why visits to the county courthouse were sometimes rare.

Those included in the sharing group were: Kenny Smith, Kalida; Marie Schmersal who lived in Columbus Grove; husband and wife, Don and Marie Kuhlman who raised their family in the Ottawa community; Violet Wagner a resident and owner of Vi's Pizza in Continental, Florence Hughes who lived in Seneca and Allen counties before making her home in Ottoville, Eleanor Schnipke who made her home in Kalida all of her life; Eileen Kemper who grew up in the Cuba community before she moved to Kalida; Mary Jane Smith formerly of Glandorf, Pat Williamson who resided in Continental; Cecila Schroeder who grew up in the Columbus Grove community just outside the Putnam County line before moving to Kalida with her husband; and Lyle Etter who lived in the Dupont community.

Mary Jane Smith recalled her first memory of the courthouse was "such a tall building" as she passed it with her folks while in Ottawa. The Courthouse was the largest building in the county and "most people had not seen a larger building," Mary Jane said. Over the years she remembered going to the Courthouse to obtain vaccinations and her marriage license. Her husband was home on furlough from military service when they were married. She recalled a vehicle title of ownership and license plates could be obtained at the same office in the courthouse and that the driver's license tests were also given from that office. Mary Jane recalled a recent trip to the title office to transfer the title of her car into her daughter's name. "She was happy but I wasn't, she commented, "That was another change in my life". Mary Jane admires the large plaques on the first floor containing the names of county veterans. "My husband's name is listed. He served in World War II but would never talk about it," she said.

Eleanor Schnipke has her family name on the Veteran Memorial as her brother died in Germany during World War II. Eleanor's experience with the Courthouse was unique when she worked for a credit bureau in Putnam County in the early years of her marriage from 1956 to 1960. "I collected the Courthouse news and my employer printed the 'Scandal Sheet'," Eleanor explained with a laugh. The publication contained information about deed transfers, loan information, court news and other information offices in the courthouse could provide. "Newspapers printed the information and people could have it sent to their homes," Eleanor said. She later went to 'beauty school' and set up a business in Vaughnsville. Many of the residents remember driving at a young age. Eleanor shared a story in which she ran into the back of another vehicle when she was driving prior to turning 16 years old. "When I returned home my Dad was yelling at me about the accident until Sheriff Arnie Potts reminded him if anyone was going to jail over this it would be him because he let me drive," Eleanor said, "He didn't say too much after that".

Another common experience was health vaccinations. The polio vaccine distribution in the early 1960s was remembered. The vaccine was given to people by way of a dose in a sugar cube. Many remembered going to a local school to receive the vaccine for their family. Those who could not attend their distribution site could visit the Health Department in the Courthouse to receive the vaccination.

All married folks remembered going to the Courthouse to get their marriage license at a time when a blood test was necessary. Many remembered fathers, husbands and brothers going to the Courthouse to register for the draft. Some were called to serve and spent years of their lives dealing with their war experiences.

Jury Duty was an experience shared by Ron Kuhlman and Eleanor Schnipke. Ron remembered he had been away from home and received his notice late. By the time he got to the courthouse on the designated day, a jury had already been selected. Eleanor was called for jury duty but did not serve which was a good thing since she was very pregnant at the time.

Cecilia Schroeder could speak to the unexpected events of being pregnant. She recalled when her first set of twins were born, one at home and the other at the hospital. "My daughter took a little bump on her head when she was born at home so when things happened to her we would tease her about the cause being the bump she took to her head," Cecilia joked.

Many of the folks joining the conversation did not live in the Ottawa area. Trips to Ottawa were seldom. There were stronger memories of being involved in their town events such as church socials and outdoor movie night. The early history of Ottawa included movie theatres but small towns including Columbus Grove, Miller City, Fort Jennings, Cloverdale and Kalida had their own movie nights when a motion picture was shown on the side of a light colored building. People sat on the ground, enjoyed the movie, and visited. Paying taxes and the Putnam County Fair were the most common reasons to visit Ottawa.

Although many of the group were from the Kalida community none could remember family members discussing the relocation of the County seat from the original Kalida location to Ottawa.

Lyle Etter remembered going to the courthouse on a regular basis during the 20 years he served as a township trustee. He organized and attended monthly meetings at the courthouse. His family shares the distinction of 100-year celebration with the Putnam County Courthouse. His mother celebrated her 100th birthday in the spring. She was born the year Putnam County government took up residence in its new home.

"Thought I was in heaven"

Memories ranged from the sublime to the destructive when a lively group of residents of the Meadows care facility in Leipsic met to share memories of the Putnam County Courthouse.

Cecilia Zeller, a former Kalida resident, remembered traveling to the Courthouse with her father when she was about 13 years old to pay taxes. "I had never been in the courthouse and thought I was in heaven when I saw it for the first time. It was so big and beautiful", Cecilia remembered. "Taxes were something that had to be paid and as soon as you paid what was due you started saving for the next tax bill," she said. As a young child Cecila remembered adults talking about the dispute concerning where the courthouse should be located. "Kalida people thought they were the center of the county and thought the courthouse should be there," she recalled.

The elevator that operated in the newly constructed courthouse was a thrill for Ferryl Billingsley who lived in Leipsic. She chuckled when she reminisced that the restrooms were something you had to take advantage of when visiting. "I remember being in the courthouse when I was younger", Ferryl said, "But a bigger memory for me was taking the street car from Leipsic to Ottawa to attend the Putnam County Fair. It was a big event back then." She also told with pride of her husband and son serving in the Coast Guard.

Ninty-one year old Aggie Mattern recalled her son registering at the courthouse for military service and serving in Korea. She too remembered the struggle concerning the location of the courthouse and talk of the cause of the fire which destroyed the first courthouse which was located in Kalida.

Mary Kuhbander formerly of Ottawa used her sense of humor when sharing that one of her more recent visits to the Courthouse was mandated by a speeding ticket. Voicing her protest she declared that she was not going that fast but told of how her children enjoyed teasing her about the ticket. Mary recalled spending time in the Courthouse with efforts to obtain birth certificates for her brothers. "Their birth was not recorded at the time they were born and it was difficult to get years later," she said. Mary also recalled her husband going to the Courthouse to register for the draft.

Bill Ziegler, a resident of Miller City area all of his life, remembered Evelyn Blossom who worked at the 'Draft Board' when he registered for military service. "I remember going to the Courthouse to register and to report for service after I was drafted," he said. He served in Korea. Bill had fond memories of going to the Armory building in Ottawa every Saturday night as a young man to dance. The Armory still stands one block from the Courthouse and serves as a county office building.

Florence Lowry lived in Pennsylvania most of her life but came to live in Leipsic to be closer to family. The 90-year-old Meadows resident proudly told of her granddaughter, Jodi Kersh, who worked for Judge Thomas Unverferth, Probate/Juvenile Judge for 14 years. Her husband's employment took them from the Putnam County area. Because of her granddaughter's involvement with the courts Florence had visited the Courthouse and thought it an attractive building that had been well kept over the years.

Ray Woods, an Ottawa resident, lived in Indiana early in his marriage. He stated he was traveling to Pandora on business when he noticed the house on the corner, across from Sts. Peter and Paul Church, was for sale. "I liked the community and told my wife we should check into the house," Ray remembered. "The house came up for auction and I purchased it for $11,000". He and his wife raised their family while living in Ottawa where his five sons graduated from Ottawa-Glandorf High School. Ray worked for St. Rita's Medical Center for 21 years and helped construct the first Putnam County Ambulatory Care Center on Williamstown Road. Ray has captured his memories in book form as he wrote about his time in Ottawa with his wife in a book entitled "Can I have this dance for the Rest of Our Lives." He also wrote a book entitled, "D-Day Hero-Destroyer" which tells of his experiences as a schooled radarman on a large naval destroyer ship that was involved in six major invasions during World War II. He was aware of the large military plaques in the Courthouse that honor all those who served but is not included in the tribute since he registered for service in Indiana. "I have attended and enjoyed the annual Memorial Day services conducted at the Courthouse," Ray stated.

"It was a privilege to use"

Memories of the past and predictions about the future were shared when a group of residents at the Putnam Heritage Care facility gathered to reminisce about the 100 years of the Putnam County Courthouse.

Eileen Winkel, 93, grew up in the small Putnam County community of Prentiss, met her husband in Leipsic and moved to Ottawa after marriage. She lived 56 years of her married life in a large white house across from the Love Funeral Home. As a child she remembered her Father being cited for bootlegging. "Someone turned him in so he had to go to the courthouse and pay a fine. It really wasn't that big of a deal at that time," she said.

Eileen told of difficult times when her son was indicted into court on drug charges. "We got through that and he is a better man today," she said. Other members of the group recalled sitting through serious court proceedings that caused their families great stress and sorrow over the years. While those were difficult times most could remember people working in the courthouse to be helpful and good to them.

Marie Alexander, a former resident of Columbus Grove, told of the court hearing when she was divorced, remembering that experience as "The best thing that happened to me". Marie also recalled the immunization shots administered at the Courthouse, especially the Small Pox vaccination that left a scab and a small scare on her arm. Putnam County health nurses Alberta Barr, Betty Stowe and Bertile Sherman were remembered as providing excellent service to county residents.

Frances Salsbury, 92, grew up in the Miller City community and later made her home with her husband on West Main St. in Ottawa. She told of her great grandfather, Joe Zink, who served as sheriff of Putnam County for many years. "He had some influence in moving the Courthouse to Ottawa," Frances said. She also stated that living in Ottawa often caused people to take the importance and grandeur of the Courthouse for granted. She remembered the enjoyment of the Saturday evening social times in the Courthouse area of Ottawa. "It was a privilege to get there," Frances stated.

Janet Weis Bhatti lived on Elm Center Road in the Ottawa community before making her home at the Heritage facility. She told of the Weis family history throughout the county. Janet wrote a thanksgiving story in 1991 about what Putnam County has to be grateful for that was published in a magazine, "Bend of the River" and in the Putnam County Sentinel. Janet voiced her speculation about what Ottawa would look like 100 years from now. "With new construction and effects of flooding, will the town's Main Street still be past the Putnam County Courthouse," she questioned.

The County Courthouse is one of those 100 year old thankful aspects of life in Putnam County. Members of this group recalled many of those blessings as displayed in the "fantastic" stained glass windows and spacious staircase which highlight the building as well as the running water restrooms in the early days which were "a privilege". Much different then an outhouse at home.

"We would always come early so my Dad could get a parking spot in front of the Courthouse"

Trips to the Putnam County Courthouse for business and for pleasure were part of stories shared by residents of the Hilty Home in Pandora.

Betsy Steiner was born and spent her childhood years in Ottawa prior to moving to Pandora. Her memories of the early days of the Courthouse were about how grand the steps, on the inside and outside of the building were. "I don't think there was a handrail on the outside steps in the early days and those inside marble steps were something. I always thought even the furniture, especially the tables, seemed large and were such fine furniture," she recalled. "The clock in front of the building is a landmark and was appreciated because you knew the time when you were near," she said and added "Our Courthouse has always looked good back then and now". Betsy remembered she was always a little leery of the elevator and usually took the steps. "I think you had to operate it yourself and I just didn't like that," she reminisced.

Betty Schaublin, a 90 year old resident, lived most of her life in the Columbus Grove community. She remembered that every Saturday night included a trip to Ottawa, to shop and socialize usually around the Courthouse. "We would always come early so that my Dad could get a parking spot right in front of the Courthouse. If he didn't get that spot he was not very happy," Betty remembered.

The ladies reminisced about activities which provided everyone something to do on the weekly trips, There were movies at two theaters, shopping at the 'Dime Store' and grocery stores, local taverns and restaurants. When the evening shopping and activities were complete most people congregated around the courthouse to socialize. "There was a water fountain on the side of the courthouse grounds next to the movie theatre. "Everyone liked that," Betty stated. Saturday evening church services were conducted on the lawn of the courthouse by ministers throughout the county which the ladies could remember attending.

Betsy remembered a time when she went to the "Dime" store on one of those Saturday night outings and bought a bag of wafer cookies for a few cents. "They tasted so good and I ate them all," she remembered and then added with a chuckle and some regret, "I didn't feel too good after that and I can't eat that type of cookies yet today".

Dorothy Moser, lived all of her life in the Pandora area. She remembered coming to the Courthouse to get her marriage license in 1947. She was married in a triple wedding ceremony in Pandora with two of her sisters on June 29, 1947, on her parents' 39th wedding anniversary. "It was a special day for all of us and our husbands", Dorothy stated. "We had a reception with ice cream and cake and I believe some little sandwiches. I remember going to Toledo to buy three identical wedding dresses and our three other sisters were our attendants. I think our parents were proud," she said. Dorothy's memory of the "Dime store" involved her son Tom. "When he was 5 years old he wanted a BB Gun and I just didn't know. I finally said he could have one if he stopped sucking his thumb. It worked!" Dorothy chuckled.

Betsy, Betty and Dorothy stated that all of their husbands are memorialized on the Military Service plaques located on the first floor of the Courthouse. They signed up for the draft at the courthouse and were summoned to the courthouse to report in for service, according to the trio. Betty could remember coming to the Draft Board to apply for benefits available to family of servicemen. Dorothy also recalled the 'location' cards they received which told where family members were stationed and where mail could be sent. She believed this information came through the draft board. A sense of pride and of duty was in her voice as she told of her husband's participation as a soldier that freed one of the concentration camps in Germany when World War II came to an end. All of the ladies stated their husbands did not speak about their war service but Betty stated her husband once said, "My parents did not bring me up to shoot people". Betsy and Dorothy both remembered when a close neighbor and classmate, Melvin Hilty, died during his service and was brought home.

All three ladies had experience with the county court system in addition to jury duty. Betsy explained that her first time in a courtroom was in her early years when she attended a hearing concerning a land dispute. Betty stated she supported her children through their divorce hearing. Dorothy remembered a time over 30 years ago when she was called as a witness concerning a rape case.

Fond memories of attending the Putnam County Fair were expressed. "If you didn't go to the fair something was wrong with you," Betty declared. She remembered a time as a child that her mother gave her and each of her siblings a quarter for a day of fun at the fair. "I saved my quarter," Betty stated. Betsy told of an aunt and uncle who lived in Ottawa. "I would ask a friend to come with me. We stayed overnight at their house and could enjoy more that one day of the fair," she said. They all agreed there were many attractions at the annual October fair and that most people dressed up when they attended.

Employed within the walls of the Courthouse:
Janet Heckman – Putnam County Treasurer's office 38 years

Janet's first recollection of the Courthouse was in her teens when her family traveled to Probate Court to sign off on her Dad's estate following his death. She came to the courthouse years later to begin working for Treasurer, Ed Heckman in 1975. Her experience in working with a Burroughs bookkeeping machine gave her the experience necessary to work in that office

Computers were introduced in the Treasurer's office with the election of Jean Quinn in 1978. Prior to that time everything was recorded, alphabetized and reconciled by hand according to Janet. The first computerization system required employees to key punch information onto cards and then run them through a noisy reader. Machinery was very large.

At one time the Treasurer's office employed four full time people. At the present time there is one full time, one part time and the Treasurer working in the office. Janet remembered the days when there was no air conditioning in the Courthouse. She recalled fans would blow papers and when trying to put thousands in alphabetical order fans were a recipe for disaster.

The scope of financial change Janet has witnessed included the following facts:

- Interest rates for the county investment money went from 21% in 1980s to 1/10% in 2012

- Interest income in 2000 was approximately $1,139,000.00 compared to $120,000.00 in 2012

- The first half real estate collection in 1972 was $1,700,000.00. First half in 2012 was $15,200,000.00

Janet recalled that as long as she worked in the Treasurer's office there was a gun stored in the office safe. Treasurer Robert Benroth donated the weapon to the Putnam County Museum in 2001. Many nostalgic items used in the Treasurer's office over the past 100 years are displayed in the entrance of the office.

Janet has an appreciation for history and antiques and has enjoyed working in the 100-year old Courthouse. She especially enjoys showing people the attic and helping them research ancestral homestead records. Duplicate records from the 1850s are stored in the attic of the Courthouse as well as books from the Kalida Courthouse which burned. Some are extensively damaged from the fire, she noted.

Some of her courthouse memories over the years include when Janitor Jerry Maidlow uncoverd the ceiling sky lights on the third floor so that natural light could enter the building. "It was a great discovery back then," she stated. The County Health Department was located where the Vehicle Title Office and the employee lunch room are located today. Janet remembered when kindergarten screening and vaccination shots were given in the Courthouse. She also recalled when the Board of Education, under the direction of Collin Stackhouse was located on the first floor of the Courthouse where the Commissioners office is today. The Commissioners were housed on the second floor in the central office as visitors walked up the steps to the second floor. The Board of Elections which is housed in the Armory Building, a block from the Courthouse, was also located on the first floor of the Courthouse where the Veteran's Administration office is located now.

Janet's family has a rich history of involvement in county employment as other family members were also employed in Courthouse offices over the years.   Her sister, Kathy Ruhe, worked in the Clerk of Courts office under Clerk, Art Beckman.   Another sister, Rose Riepenhoff, worked in the Auditor's office under Eppie Hoffman in the 1970s.

Jeannie Selhorst – Putnam County Auditor's office 26 years

During her employment in the Putnam County Auditor's office Jeannie Selhorst has seen advancement into the computer age. The key punch recording system was removed in the early 1980's when computers became part of the office décor. Jeannie remember the server at that time was a Burroughs measuring five feet tall, two feet deep and six feet long. Backup was completed with a one- half inch reel tape. According to Jeannie the Burroughs was replaced in the early 1990s with an IBM AS400. This was upgraded over the years until an IBM 520 Power System replaced the Auditor's office system in 2010. Jeannie stated "We now backup the entire system with a cartridge the size of a cassette tape.

Microfilming of paper records has changed business processes and storage needs in the Auditor's office. In 2000 the office started microfilming payroll records back to 1967. "An average year of pay histories for all employees took approximately four microfilm sheets," Jeannie stated compared to paper copies that filled two large ledger books, usually five sheets per employee. The system was again modernized in 2007 when the records began to be stored digitally instead of by microfilm. All payroll today is recorded on one CD, Jeannie started

Another area Jeannie has seen constant change is in the area of providing insurance for county employees. She reported that a family hospitalization policy cost $641.69 in 1989 compared to a cost of $1,590.99 today.

One of Jeannie's favorite memories involved a janitorial couple, Carolyn and Norbert Karhoff, who took care of the Courthouse along with Jerry Maidlow. She recalled returning from lunch one day to find Carolyn setting on the inside steps of the building cleaning the dirt from the cracks between marble with an old toothbrush. Carolyn thought it was the best way to remove all the dirt. Jerry and Norbert were as meticulous with their work as they would often stand on outside ledges of the building to clean windows. "Their dedication to the upkeep of the building was commendable," Jean stated.

X. HISTORY PANELS TRAVELING EXHIBIT

A group of twelve 24" x 30" pictorial panels were compiled in June of 2013 to document the progress of Putnam County, Ohio from its organization in 1834 through the building of the courthouse, 1909-1913. They are titled:

Establishing Putnam County

The Petition

Building Commission

Architecture

Innovations of Design and Construction

Construction

Beaux Arts Interior

The Courthouse Cost

Workers

Courts

Back in the Day ...

Offices

This traveling exhibit first appeared in the Putnam County Historical Society booth at the June 24-29, 2013 Putnam County Fair. Additional appearances are scheduled throughout Putnam County during 2013.

ESTABLISHING PUTNAM COUNTY

Original Document - Putnam County was named for Israel Putnam who served as a general in the Revolutionary War in America. On May 5, 1834 Putnam County was organized with its own jurisdiction. William Cochran, Henry Morris, and Silas McClish, associate judges appointed by Ohio governor Robert Lucas, met at the home of Abraham Sarber, Union Township, where they appointed the first county officials.

> Court of Common Pleas of Putnam County May Term 1834
> At a Court of Common Pleas begun and held for the Court of Putnam at the dwelling house of Abraham Sarber in said county on the fifth day of May in the year of our lord one thousand eight hundred and thirty four and of the State of Ohio the thirty third.

Courthouses - The first courthouse was a temporary frame building built 1834-1835 in Kalida, the county seat. In 1838-1839 an imposing red brick building was constructed, also in Kalida

A vote of the people in 1866 named Ottawa as the county seat. By December 1866 the site for the first courthouse in Ottawa was decided. Construction started on the two-story building in May 1867. By the end of December 1867 all of the county officials were occupying their offices in the new red brick courthouse on East Main Street.

In 1902 questions arose about replacing the courthouse because of structural problems. A petition signed by 500 citizens was presented to the Board of Commissioners asking that the issue of a levy for construction of a new couthouse be placed before the voters. The voters turned it down - 1,659 for and 4,017 against.

In 1909 a petition seeking a levy to build a new courthouse was again presented to the Board of County Commissioners. At a special election held September 7, 1909 the official vote for a new courthouse resulted in 2,825 for the proposal with 2,129 against the proposal. The contractors began work on June 24, 1910 and the building was accepted by the board May 21, 1912. By December 1912 all but one of the county elected officials were in their new offices.

1835 Kalida

PUTNAM COUNTY'S FIRST COURT HOUSE.

1848 Kalida (No photo/drawing located)

1867 Ottawa

1912 Ottawa Before retaining walls and sidewalks

The Petition

Prominent citizen Ezra Warren filed a petition with names from across Putnam County seeking a vote for the construction of a new courthouse. A similar vote several years before had been defeated, but the State of Ohio had subsequently issued an order condemning the old building because of structural issues. The new petition provided for a total construction cost of no more than $250,000 and became a referendum on whether to build a new courthouse or repair the old one.

Five hundred citizens signed a petition to the County Commissioners on August 9th, 1909, seeking a vote for a new Courthouse.

The Putnam County Sentinel became one of the biggest proponents of building a new courthouse, pointing out the past fires at the Kalida courthouse and suggesting that proof of ownership of farms and houses was at risk if a new fire proof building was not built.

Graffiti on the day following the voter's approval of a new courthouse tagged the old building as 'a thing of the past'.

The Commissioners reduced the amount of the proposed construction to $200,000 and placed the issue before the voters. A farmer owning 40 acres valued at $30 an acre would pay about $1.50 per year for 20 years. An anonymous circular issued days before the election stated that both the Commissioners and the Judge were corrupt and were intent on stealing more money from the taxpayers for construction. However, the argument that the old building was unusable carried the day and the voters approved the measure 57% to 43%.

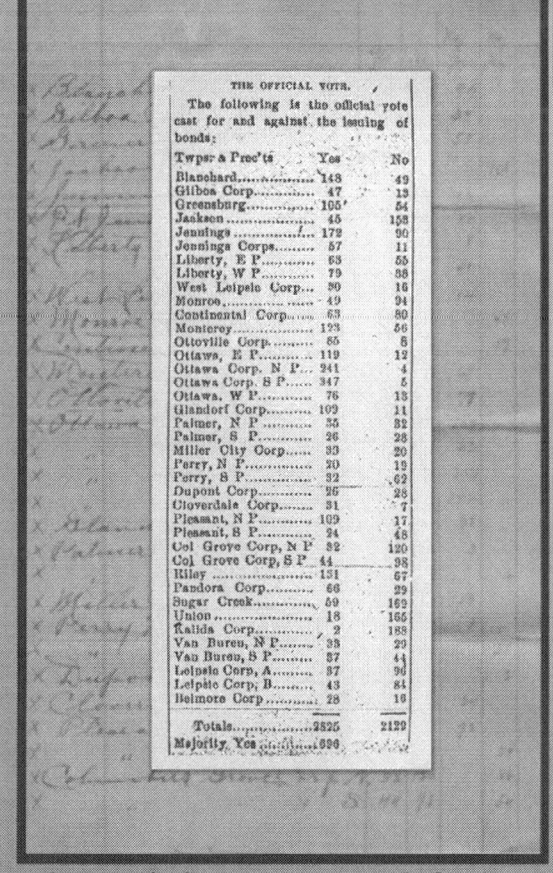

THE OFFICIAL VOTE.

The following is the official vote cast for and against the issuing of bonds:

Twps. & Prec'ts	Yes	No
Blanchard	148	49
Gilboa Corp	47	13
Greensburg	105	54
Jackson	45	158
Jennings	172	90
Jennings Corp	57	11
Liberty, E P	65	55
Liberty, W P	79	88
West Leipsic Corp	80	16
Monroe	49	94
Continental Corp	63	80
Monterey	123	56
Ottoville Corp	85	5
Ottawa, E P	119	12
Ottawa Corp, N P	241	4
Ottawa Corp, S P	347	5
Ottawa, W P	76	13
Glandorf Corp	109	11
Palmer, N P	55	82
Palmer, S P	26	28
Miller City Corp	33	20
Perry, N P	20	19
Perry, S P	32	62
Dupont Corp	25	28
Cloverdale Corp	31	7
Pleasant, N P	109	17
Pleasant, S P	24	45
Col Grove Corp, N P	82	120
Col Grove Corp, S P	44	98
Riley	151	67
Pandora Corp	66	29
Sugar Creek	59	162
Union	18	155
Kalida Corp	2	188
Van Buren, N P	35	29
Van Buren, S P	37	44
Leipsic Corp, A	87	96
Leipsic Corp, B	43	84
Belmore Corp	28	16
Totals	2825	2129
Majority Yes	696	

Vote totals show strong support in Ottawa and little support in Kalida to construct a new courthouse.

BUILDING COMMISSION

A building commission was established following the September 1909 election which favored replacing the 1867 Court House in Ottawa. County Commissioners Bernard A. Ruhe, Pleasant Township; Jacob Bright, Van Buren Township; and Jacob Best, Pleasant Township, were joined on the commission by four other men appointed by Common Pleas Judge John P. Bailey. These men were
Judge Julius S. Ogan, Sr., Ottawa; Joseph C. Wannemacher, Ottoville businessman; Dr. Warren F. Reed, president Bank of Ottawa; and Peter B. Hilty, Pandora businessman.
In April the Court House Building Commission accepted the working plans for the new Court House from architect Frank Lucius Packard, Columbus, Ohio. Born in Delaware, Ohio in 1866, Mr. Packard was one of America's foremost institutional architects, designing over 3,400 buildings, including over 100 business and residential buildings in Columbus alone. He also drafted one of the first master plans
for the Ohio State University in Columbus.

Contract
Frank L. Packard
Architect
11 December 1909

Whereas on the 11th day of December, 1909, the Building Commission, for the erection of a new Court House in Putnam County, Ohio, and a heating and ventilating plant therefor, to be erected upon the site of the present Court House in Ottawa, Ohio, and the property of the County adjacent thereto, did appoint one Frank L. Packard, architect of Columbus, Ohio, to assist the said Commission as architect.

Now, therefore, it is agreed between the said Frank L. Packard, architect of Columbus, Ohio, hereinafter designated as party of the first part, and the said Building Commission hereinafter designated as party of the second part, as follows:-

In Witness Whereof the parties to these presents have hereunto set their hands this 11th day of December, 1909.

Frank L. Packard
Architect.

The Court House Building Commission
by *B. A. Rieke*
Jacob Bright
Jacob Best
W. B. Reed
J. C. Agan
D. C. Wannemacher
Peter B. Hilty
Members of Building Commission.

Written and signed in duplicate:-
WITNESSES:
W. Frick
Joseph Kersting

The foregoing contract is approved
Frank
Prosecuting Attorney

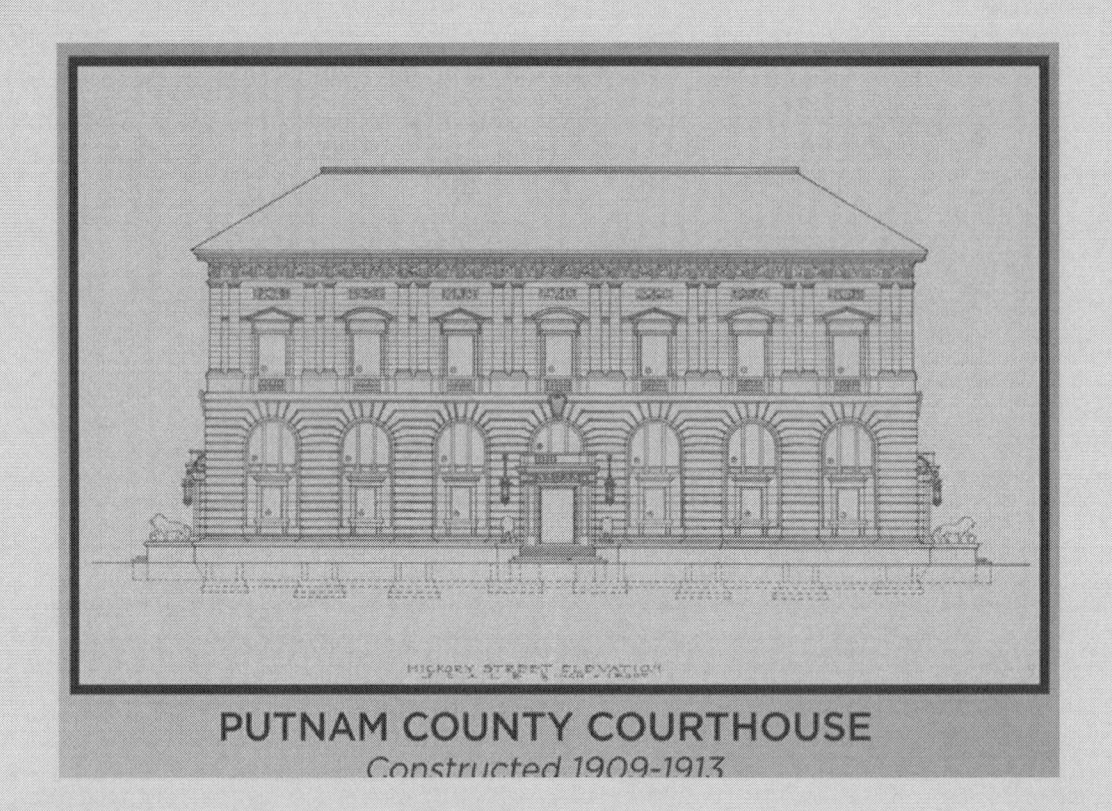

Architecture

PUTNAM COUNTY COURTHOUSE
Constructed 1909-1913

Columbus architect Frank Packard designed the Courthouse in an Italian Renaissance style common to the period. Packard designed three thousand public buildings including four courthouses in Ohio and much of the early Ohio State University campus including the oval and library. The building design was a 'post civil war Italian influence' common at the turn of the 20th century. Beaux-Arts style completes the interior of the building including intricate molding, stained glass, and wood carvings.
Columbus architect Frank Packard designed the Courthouse in an Italian Renaissance style common to the period. Packard designed three thousand public buildings including four courthouses in Ohio and much of the early Ohio State University campus including the oval and library. The building design was a 'post civil war Italian influence' common at the turn of the 20th century. Beaux-Arts style completes the interior of the building including intricate molding, stained glass, and wood carvings.
The outside appearance of the building includes a visual appearance of a two story building capped with a Roman clay tile roof. A mansard roof in the center of the building covers the skylight system for the Common Pleas Courtroom and central hallway. Horizontal lines and curved arches of the outer façade are typical of an Italian Renaissance design. Double columns, inset balconies with balustrades, and alternating rounded and peaked inset arches predominate on the upper floor. Deep openings, heavy walls, and carved stone complete the outer appearance. A two foot high retaining wall surrounds the courthouse block to provide a setback and added dimension,

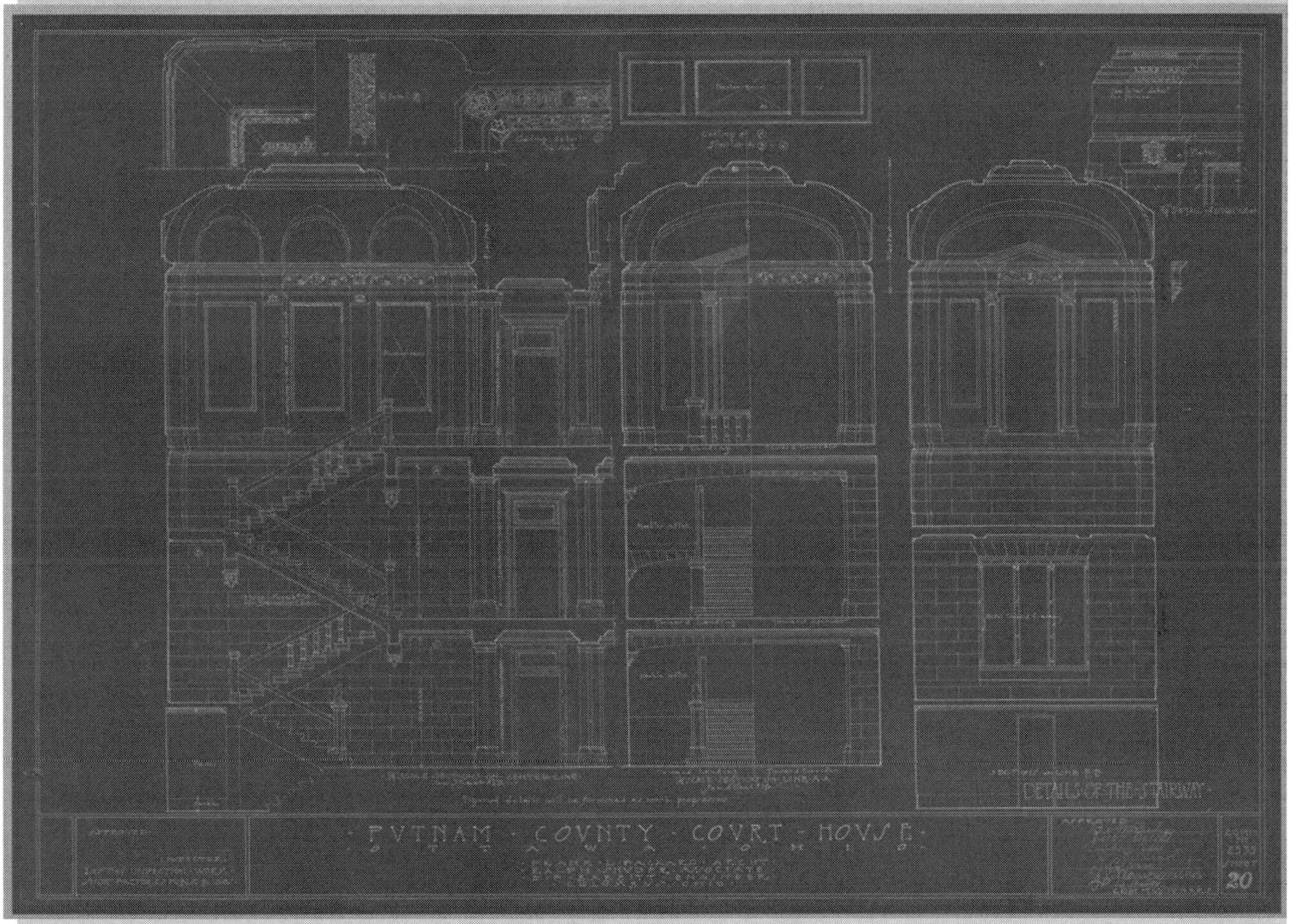
PUTNAM · COUNTY · COURT · HOUSE
DETAILS OF THE STAIRWAY
20

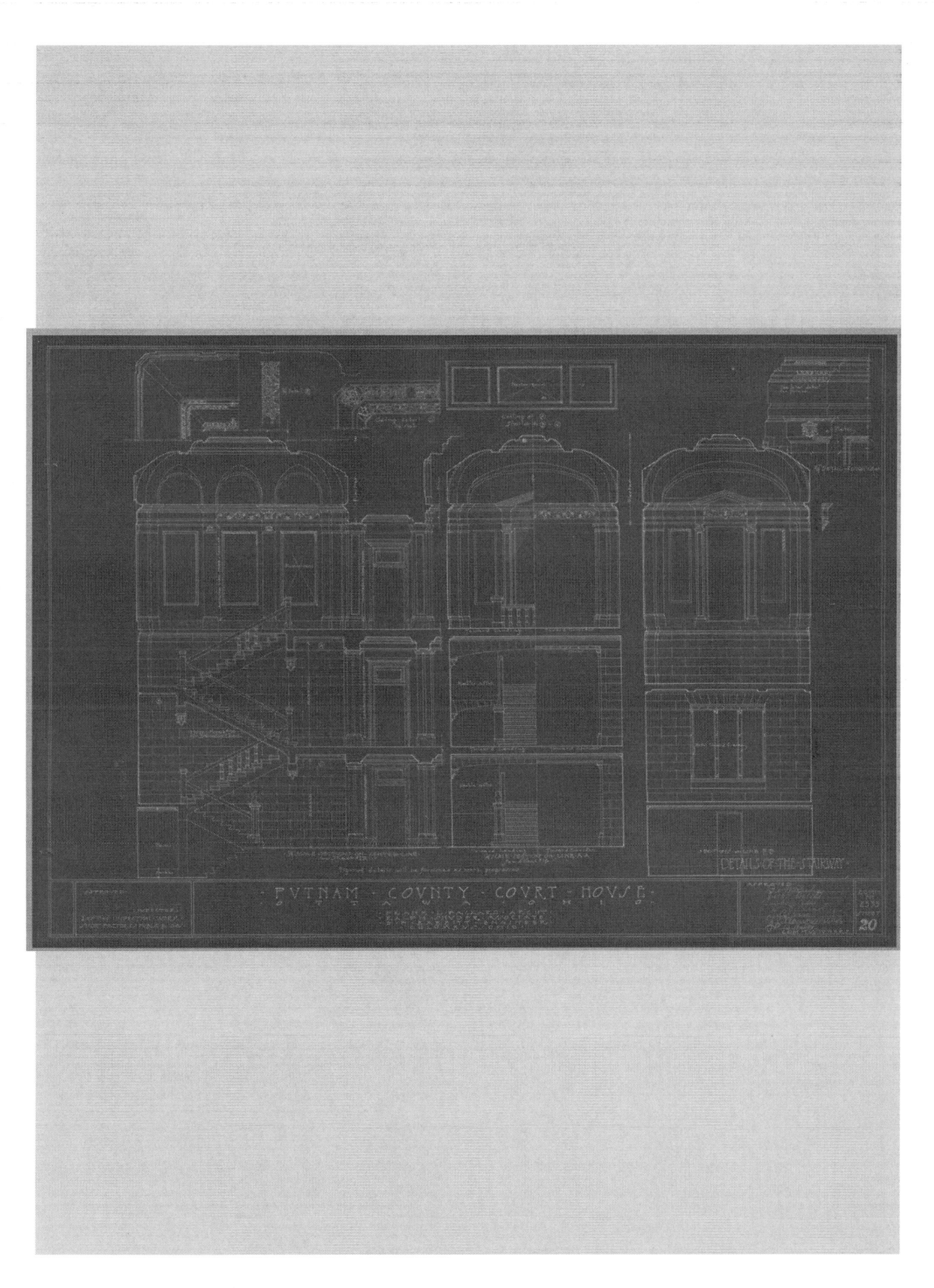

Construction

Construction continues on December 15th, 1910 on the east side of the Courthouse. Workers place limestone blocks on wood frames in the window openings. Steel beams centered the building and the milled stone exterior was set in concrete mortar prepared in cement mixers seen in the foreground. The photo to the right shows the finished east side as displayed in Architectural Review in 1914. Photo courtesy of Matthew Cunningham

General Contractor R.H. Evans of Zanesville was the low bidder and was awarded a contract for construction at a cost of $198,290, and the building was built for that amount. Evans used skilled workmen brought in for the project from other parts of the state as well as some local laborers.
Construction specifications were submitted by the architect and approved by the seven members of the Courthouse Building Commission. The specifications and blue prints detailed all aspects of construction and the materials to be used, often stating the company in Ohio or the mid-west where the materials were to be obtained. Materials were brought by train to one of the three rail lines serving Ottawa and transferred by horse and wagon or truck to the courthouse block. A six foot solid wood fence surrounded the building during construction.
A granite stone foundation and limestone outer walls enclosed the steel frame of the building. Red semi glazed Roman roof tiles were attached with two tinned nails each and covered a storm proof roof leading to copper gutters.

Bronzed doors stood inside iron pocket doors on the entrances to the Courthouse.

Prism glass panels on the roof directed light to the third floor skylights of the courtrooms and hallway below.

BEAUX ARTS INTERIOR

Skilled workmen on scaffolding near the ceiling of the Common Pleas Courtroom attached ornamental plaster under the skylights.

Paintings on mesh covered mortar panels overlook the central staircase.

The ornamental works and moldings were of mortar lime paste, sand, and sufficient quantity of cow hair to insure a good bond. Plastered moldings were built using a carved mold impressed over the mortar by workers on site. Central skylights found in the Common Pleas
Courtroom were built in floor frames with the cow haired mortar hardened and then put in place with a rope and pulley system and fixed to the ceiling. The attic includes a second skylight system twenty feet above the interior skylights with end glazed prisms to deflect natural light to the central hallway and main courtroom.

Elaborate ornamental moldings were created with the detailed specifications of the Architect.

Wood used through the building was quarter sawed white oak, stained and finished with linseed oil. Carvings and woodworking were done to specification off site and shipped.
Plans called for many of the materials to be manufactured by specific companies located in Ohio and the Midwest.

WORKERS

Robert H. Evans & Company was the general contractor when ground was broken for the court house in June 1910. Local residents worked on the building as well as skilled tradesmen. Two Ottawa firemen were killed in January 1911 at a fire on East Second Street. Several others were injured as they went to the scene to help. "All were Ottawa residents with the exception of Harry Catle who was employed on the court house then in the course of construction."

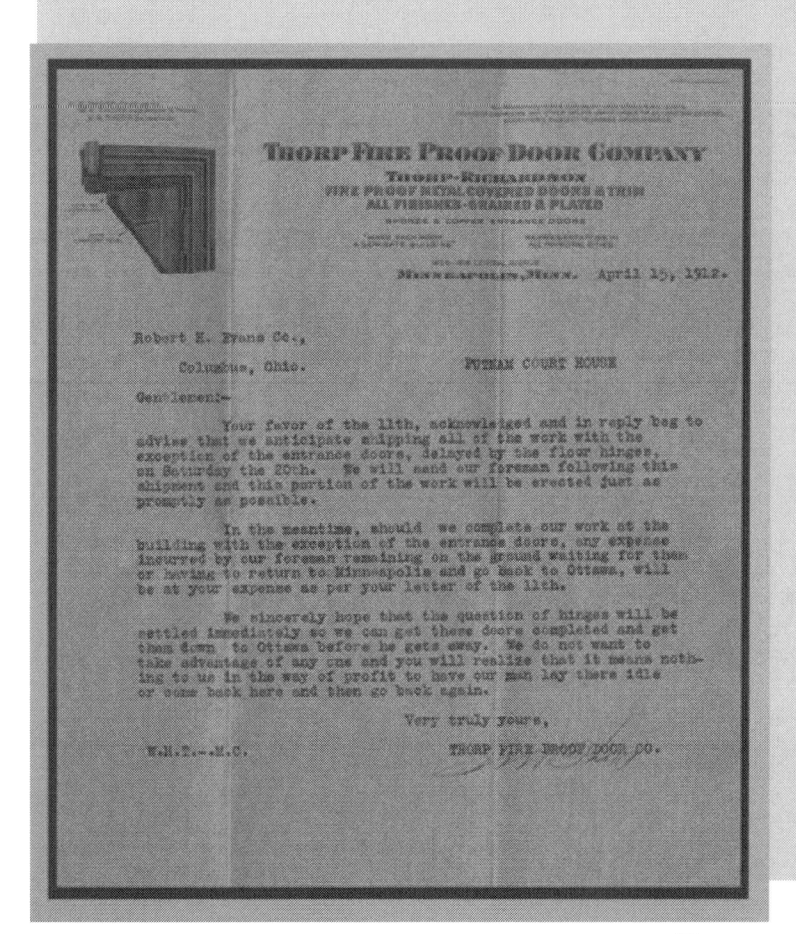

As construction progressed some changes were made in the plans. For example, Robert H. Evans proposed "to furnish marble in place of Caen stone finish in the corridors, using all Tennessee marble throughout the building including floors, in place of marble specified, for the sum of $8000.00"

By April 1912, in a letter to Robert H. Evans, the building commission was concerned that "occupancy of the new court house" was delayed because the metal and fireproof doors were not yet in place. Evans replied that "the delay in furnishing and placing these doors has been caused by the failure of your Board to furnish the hardware for same and also by reason of the furnishing of the hardware which was not suitable to be applied to the doors when it was furnished." The doors were purchased from Thorp Fire Proof Door Company, Minneapolis, MN.

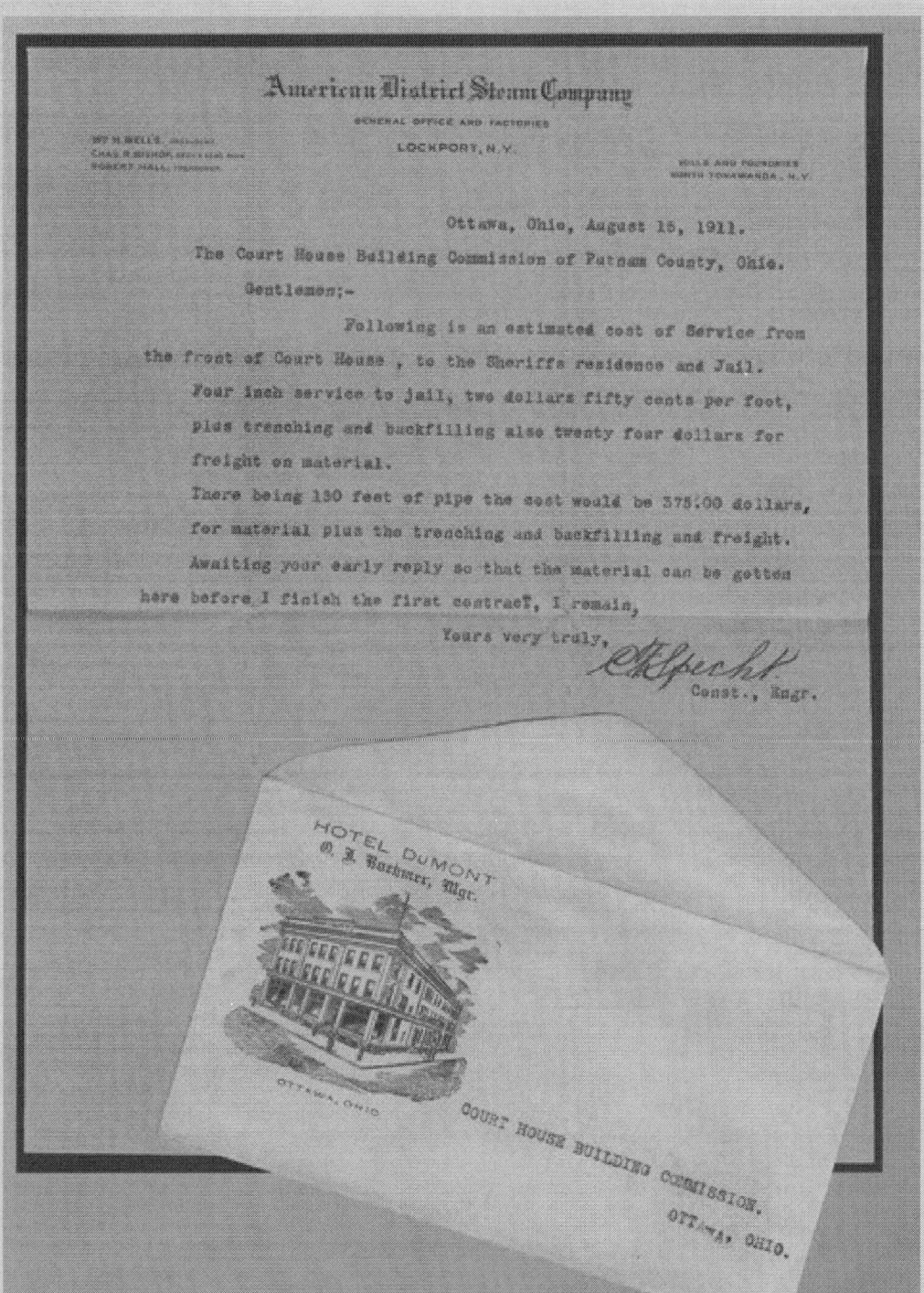

THE COURTHOUSE COST

The original petition for the construction of the Courthouse provided for a construction amount up to $250,000. The Commissioners reviewed other construction projects in the state and put the issue to the voters in an amount not to exceed $200,000, suggesting that the actual amount could even be less. The issue of fraud and corruption in other state public works projects was debated during the election and some argued that the ultimate cost would actually exceed $700,000. The voter approval of the new courthouse included clear instructions to the Building Commission to stay within the approved amount. Construction costs at the time were relatively low, bids came in under the set amount and the building was completed for $198,290.40.

Farmland at the time of construction sold for approximately $30 per acre and a 40 acre farm resulted in taxes of about $1.25 per year, or a $25 total over a 20 year period. A comparable levy based upon today's tax evaluation would generate revenue of $13 million.

A Courthouse bond, issued payable in 15 years at 4% interest.

Workers at the time of construction earned from twenty to forty cents per hour, depending upon their skill level. A comparison to today's wages would result in the cost of the building being approximately $20-$25 million. Comparable prices for goods at the time included potatoes at two cents a pound, a hotel room for a dollar, taking the train for ten cents, or a stamp for one cent.

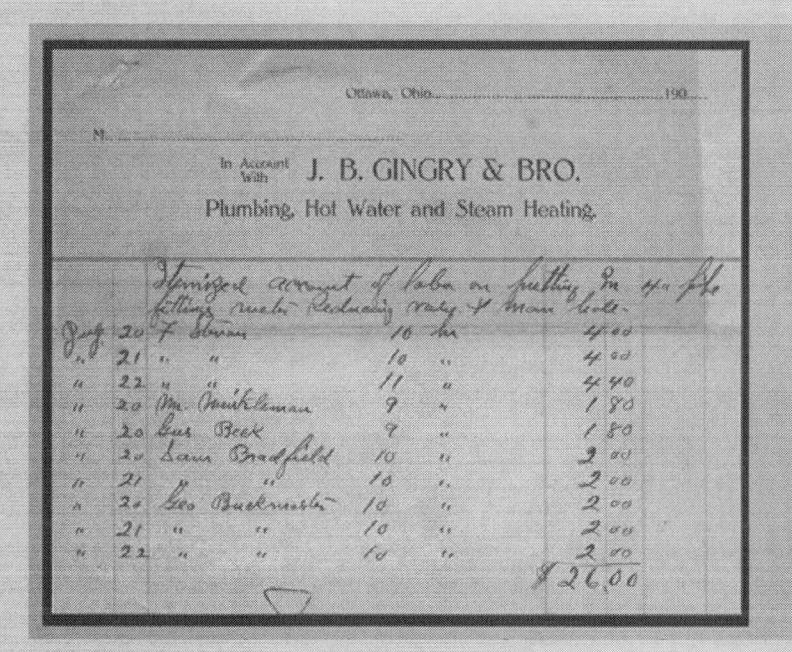

An invoice shows labor costs of twenty or forty cents per hour for Courthouse construction workers, based upon skill levels.

Farmland and labor costs were relatively low compared to today, while many consumer or technological goods o the time were higher in comparison. The cost of the Courthouse in today's dollars would be about $60 million if compared to the rise in farmland prices.

farmland prices.

Courts

The first Putnam County Court was created in 1834 with the document that organized the County. Circuit judges and attorneys originally rode horseback from neighboring counties to hear cases until a full-time Common Pleas judgeship was established. A Probate-Juvenile Court was later organized, and a Municipal Court was subsequently created for misdemeanors and lesser civil cases.

An occasional murder case was heard in the Courhouse. At the previous Courthouse, an 1874 case for the double murder of a husband-and-wife resulted in the execution of the defendant on the north lawn of the existing Courthouse. The old Courthouse was the scene of the trial, and the conviction was followed by a notice in the Sentinel that a hanging would occur on the Courthouse lawn. Thousands of people came to town to watch the execution, but the Judge at the last minute ordered that fencing block the view of the actual hanging.

A triple murder in 1923 also focused media attention on the present Courthouse. A farmhand by the name of Charles Shank lived with the Tenwalde family near Kalida. The thirty year old Shank fell in love and fathered a child with 16-year-old Olivia. The family discouraged a marriage because of age and religious differences and the child was born at a Cincinnati home for unwed mothers. Shank was later spurned by Olivia and he appeared at the Tenwalde home with a gun on Pioneer weekend of 1923 and murdered Olivia, her mother, and a cousin. A subsequent manhunt for Shank resulted in his capture and trial in the Common Pleas Court. The defense claimed that Shank had a 'brainstorm', in a modified insanity defense. The jury, including women who had recently obtained the right to vote, convicted Shank of aggravated murder but rejected the death penalty and imposed a life sentence. He later died in prison. The Courts continue to hear signification legal matters involving crime, divorce, and money actions for the County. Illegal moonshine cases from the 1920s changed to illegal drug trafficking cases in recent decades. Nearly every citizen of every generation has been affected in some manner by decisions in the County Courthouse.

John Goodman was convicted of a double murder and executed on the courthouse lawn.

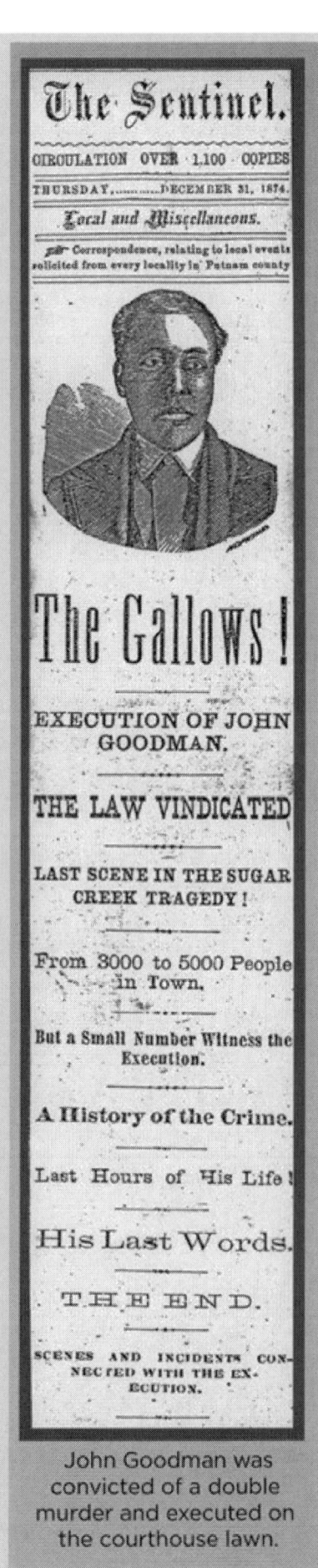

The Common Pleas Courtroom hears felonies, divorces, and major civil cases. Photos of past Judges line the wall. The room is decorated with ornamental garlands of fruit and flowers, sculptured cherubs, lion's heads, and a repeated theme of twelve. The number twelve represents twelve jurors.

Charles Shank was convicted of aggravated murder and sentenced to life in prison.(News)

(Top picture)Today's Municipal Court was originally designed for the Grand Jury.

(Bottom picture) The Probate-Juvenile Court on the second floor of the Courthouse.

INNOVATIONS OF DESIGN AND CONSTRUCTION

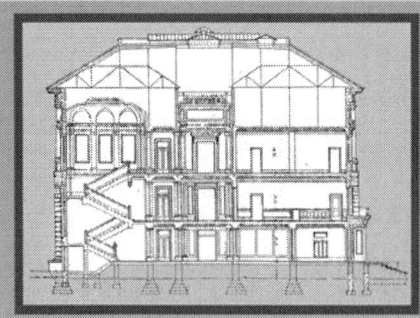

A frame steel skeleton sits on a granite foundation.

Steel framing and original ductwork are shown in the attic directly below roof pyramid glass designed to focus light onto the skylights. Each of the dozens of blue print designs was approved by the state inspector, the architect, and the seven members of the Courthouse Commission.

Architect Packard encouraged the steam line to be run from the Ottawa Power House to the Courthouse, common in large public buildings of the time.

Each of the rooms and hallways called for a specific type of marble, shown extensively here in the men's restroom, where many county residents experienced their first indoor flush toilet.

Architect Packard encouraged the steam line to be run from the Ottawa Power House to the Courthouse, common in large public buildings of the time.

Brick streets, horses, and buggies were giving way to electricity, cars, and telephones in the era of Courthouse construction. Ottawa became the first town in Putnam County to be electrified in 1890 and the Courthouse was designed with electric lighting and an elevator driven by an electric motor. Newspaper articles at the time referred to the elevator as an 'up and down wagon' and concluded that many wished they had walked rather than take this new fangled way of going up and down stairs.

Advances in steel framed construction, ventilation systems, and indoor plumbing led to integrated infrastructure designs still in use. Heat was first provided as exhaust steam piped several blocks from the Ottawa owned light plant. Coal was later used, discoloring the building.

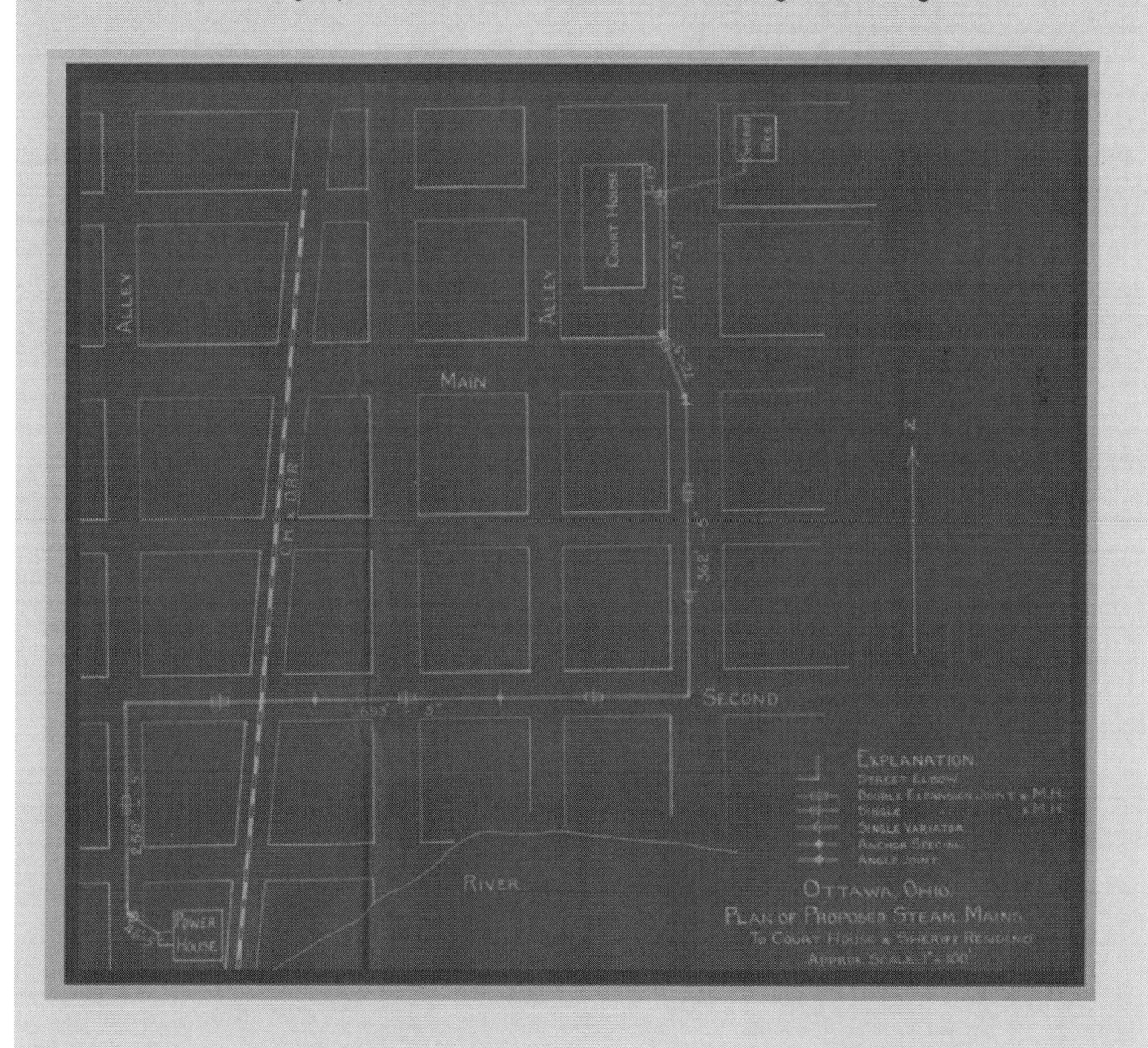

Offices

Elected Officials	1913	2013
County Commissioners	George Herman	Vincent T. Schroeder
	John R. Forney	John E. Love
	Frank H. Kracht	Travis A. Jerwers
Judge of the Court of Common Pleas -General Division	John P. Bailey	Randall L. Basinger
Judge of the Court of Common Pleas -Probate/Juvenile	Joseph Mersman	Michael A. Borer
Municipal Court Judge	(formerly County Court)	Chad C. Niese
County Auditor	John E. Roose	Robert L. Benroth
County Clerk of Courts	William M. George	Teresa J. Lammers
County Coroner	Albert F. Sheibley	Anna M. Horstman
County Engineer	James D. Cartwright	Terrence R. Recker
County Prosecuting Attorney	Josiah W. Smith	Gary L. Lammers
County Recorder	Theodore Heckman	Cathy S. Recker
County Sheriff	Nicholas F. Miller	Michael C. Chandler
County Treasurer	Frank J. Kohls	Tracy L. Warnecke

On December 13, 1912, an article in the Putnam County Sentinel stated that there was a difference of opinion about what date should be listed on commemorative plaques that would be placed in the new Court House. The Board of Commissioners considered whether the date should be June 24, 1910 when construction was started, whether it should be May 21, 1912 when the building was accepted from the contractor, or when it was first occupied for official business which was December 1912.

The plaques were ordered in the spring of 1914 from the W. S. Tyler Company, Cleveland. They were wall-mounted in the East Main Street foyer and remain there in 2013.

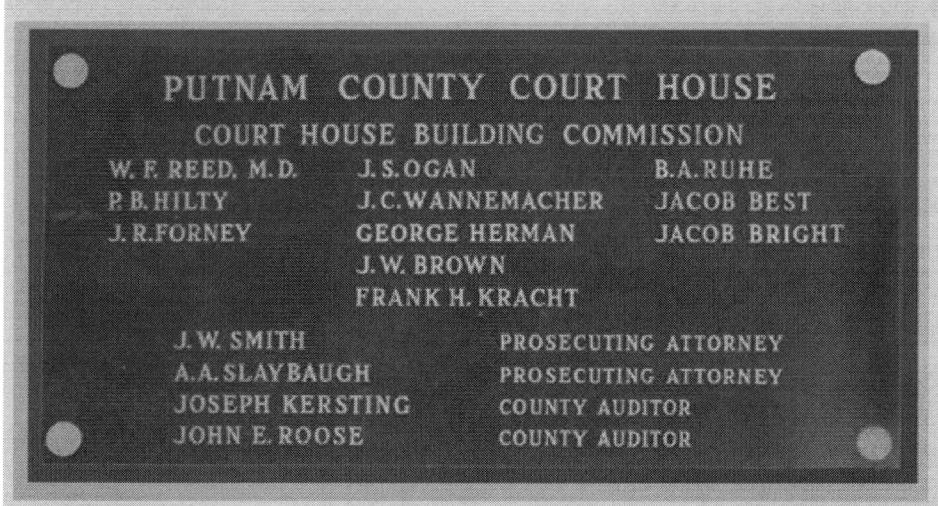

PUTNAM COUNTY COURT HOUSE
COURT HOUSE BUILDING COMMISSION

W. F. REED, M.D.	J. S. OGAN	B. A. RUHE
P. B. HILTY	J. C. WANNEMACHER	JACOB BEST
J. R. FORNEY	GEORGE HERMAN	JACOB BRIGHT
	J. W. BROWN	
	FRANK H. KRACHT	

J. W. SMITH	PROSECUTING ATTORNEY
A. A. SLAYBAUGH	PROSECUTING ATTORNEY
JOSEPH KERSTING	COUNTY AUDITOR
JOHN E. ROOSE	COUNTY AUDITOR

PUTNAM COUNTY COURT HOUSE
ERECTED 1909-1913

FRANK L. PACKARD	E. F. BABBITT
ARCHITECT	MECHANICAL EQUIPMENT
RALPH SNYDER	G. E. SWEENEY
ASSOCIATE ARCHITECT	SUPERINTENDENT

R. H. EVANS & COMPANY BUILDERS

COST $198,290.40.

When the terms of County Commissioners Jacob Best, Jacob Bright, and Bernard A. Ruhe expired they were followed in office by George Herman, John R. Forney, and Frank H. Kracht. John W. Brown, an Ottawa merchant, was appointed to the building commission following the death of Dr. Warren E. Reed.

> The Putnam County Court House History Panels were written by Judge Randall Basinger and former Putnam County Auditor and historian Roselia Deters Verhoff. They were designed by Nate Huber of Phantasm Designs. The Court House Centennial Commission, appointed February 7th, 2013, also included Clerk of Courts Teresa Lammers, Recorder Cathy Recker, Commissioner John Love, and local historians Nancy Kline, Ruth Wilhelm, Bruce Stowe, and Betty Wannemacher. Additional photos were provided by Eric Wilhem and Becky Leaderr

Back in the Day...

Health Clinics

Dr. W. S. Yeager, the County Health Commissioner conducted a diagnostic clinic for children of the county in the ladies waiting room of the Courthouse in Ottawa 1921. There was no charge for these services. The Board of Health cooperated with the Putnam County Medical Society.

It was announced in 1922 that a clinic for the "purpose of performing minor surgical operations" would be opened in the Courthouse. Donations of beds and bedding were received. On May 5, 1922 the first six operations were performed for the removal of diseased tonsils and adenoids. Ladies appointed by the president of Kiwanis Club worked tirelessy to prepare bandages, nightgowns, and other items needed by the patients, and in getting the operating room and beds ready. Beds and money were donated by local organizations such as the Knights of Columbus, the Masonic Lodge, Eastern Star, C.L. of C., Centennial Book Club, Study Club, and Odd Fellows. The operating room, believed to be on the first floor, had a table, electric sterilizer, instrument table, and other accessories "necessary for the complete operating room."

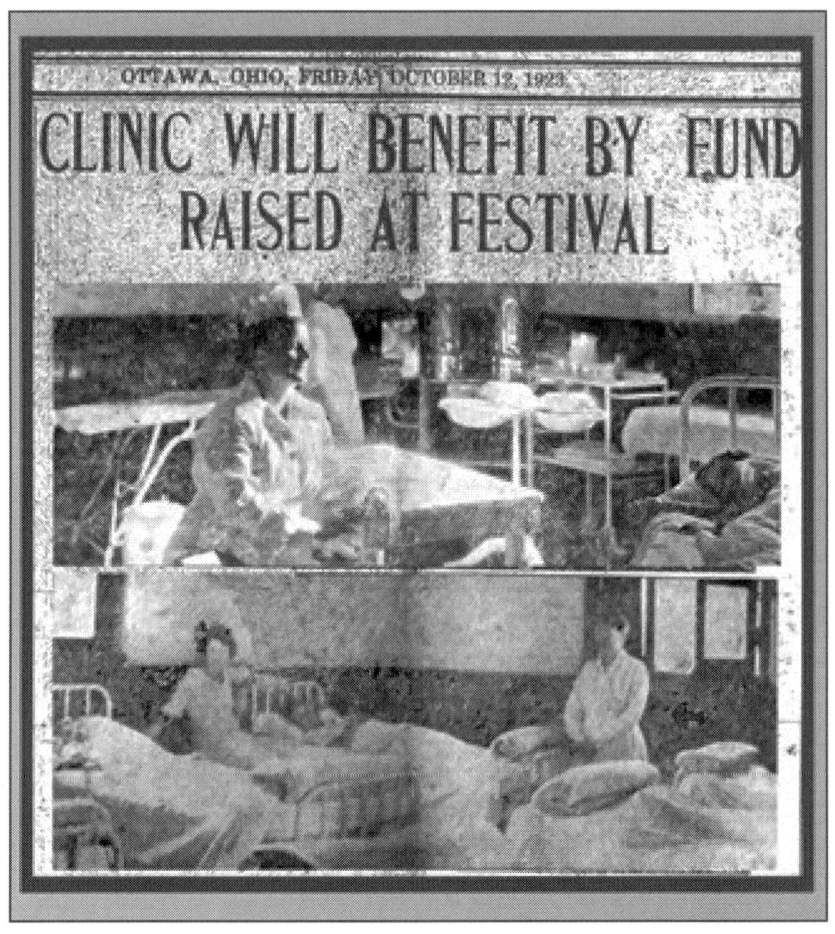

July of 1922 thirty-four operations had been performed on children for the removal of tonsils and adenoids. The tonsil clinic operated "continually for 22 years until 1943 when it had to be discontinued due to the fact that so many doctors entered militaryservice during World War II."

Public Library in Courthouse

An article titled a "Public Library for County" appeared in The Putnam County Sentinel dated February 8, 1924. It was to be located in the anteroom of the ladies' rest room on the second floor of the Putnam County Courthouse. Books that had been donated for the library by several residents would be the beginning of the collection. The County Commissioners donated used shelves and tables that were once in the county's law library.

Six ladies representing local literary clubs started the movement. Librarian services were offered by other women and girls so that the library could be open "every afternoon from one to five."

Books could also be obtained by mail. The library services were free but the person requesting a book was expected to pay the postage. Card parties, a library carnival, an Easter festival, a "book shower" and other events were held at the Armory on East Main Street, Ottawa to raise operating funds.

By the fall of 1928 the library had moved to the first floor of the courthouse. It remained there until 1934 when it moved to the corner of East Main and Locust

The Military Draft: Selective Service

The draft, sometimes called conscription, was established in 1917. This act required male citizens of the United States, and other male persons who were in the United States and were between the ages of eighteen and a half and twenty-six, to register for possible military service.

Conscription dates back to colonial times. The United States used a draft since the Civil War until 1973 when the U.S. armed services became volunteer forces. At that time the standby system took effect. In 1975 registration requirements were revamped and most remaining local boards became inactive. During the 1940's registration and notification of a call to active duty was handled by five men who served without compensation. This was known as the draft board and a local lady, named by the board, served as clerk.

Photo caption: 1945 — Original Roster Location

Veteran's Roster on First Floor

In October 1949 it was announced that the panels of veterans' names, which originally stood on the southeast corner of the courthouse lawn, would be moved into the building. The large plates of black glass listed the names of Putnam County armed service veterans.

This project was done with the cooperation of the veterans organizations and Weather-Seal Manufacturing. Because the original lettering on the black glass had weathered and deteriorated the names needed repainted. When this was completed Weather-Seal volunteered--and did--place red wood frames around the glass-covered roster panels. The newly framed panels were then attached to the hallway walls on the first floor of the courthouse.

At one time Weather-Seal constructed wooden doors and storm windows in their plant on East Second Street, Ottawa.

EPILOGUE

The Courthouse Building Commission held its last meeting in May 1914. Even though there were some controversies and some changes in plans, they had fulfilled their duties pertaining to the building of the new Courthouse.

Judge John P. Bailey, of the Court of Common Pleas, placed upon the records of the court the following certificate:

"In the matter of the compensation of the members of the Court House Building Commission, the undersigned has received the following certificate: 'State of Ohio, County of Putnam, SS. The undersigned county auditor of Putnam County hereby certifies that according to the records of the Court House Building Commission of said county in my office, the said building commission has expended a total of $211,352.98.' John E. Roose, Auditor"

At the time of the appointment of the Commission Judge John P. Bailey, acting under statutory authority, fixed the compensation of the appointed members at 2 1/2 percent of the amount disbursed by the Commission. This amounted to $1321.57 to each appointed member. This amount was certified to Auditor Roose who issued his warrant on County Treasurer Charles E. Kohls.

"The building and equipment of the new Court House have required great care and considerable time. But in the opinion of the undersigned Judge, the accomplished result is a sufficient justification for both the labor and time consumed. And each and every member of the Commission, including the different County Commissioners who have served with the appointed members, is hereby especially commended for care, diligence, and good faith. ...
    And now with the hearty thanks and best wishes of the undersigned, the Commission is finally discharged with honors."

John P. Bailey
Common Pleas Judge

Pictures from the Past

1917 - World War I war bond rally in front of the courthouse

Courthouse staff in 1942

front row (left)   Carl Frick, County Auditor.   A.A.Slaybaugh, Common Pleas Judge, Wm. George, Probate Judge

back row - Harold Maag, Sheriff Arnold Potts and Arnold Lauer, County Treasurer - others not identified

Seated in center - Mary Sheeley,   Harriet Core Frick, 2nd from right.   Standing back row: Bertille Schuerman, Health Dept. Nurse,   Lucy Cartwright, Julia Kersting and far right Mary Margaret Kahle.   Others not identified.

County officials being sworn in by Judge Mittlekamp including, Front, l-r) Dan Gerschutz, Jim Niese, Terry Recker, Martin Kuhlman, Jean Quinn and back) Dr. Overmier, Huntsman, Karl Miller, Dick Schroeder, Ron Diemer, . ? and Clair Huntsmen

Oath of office being administered by Judge Weaver (at right) to (front, l-r) Prosecuting attorney Henry Mittlekamp, Clerk of Courts Arthur Beckman, Engineer Richard Recker, Recorder Amanda Lighthill and (back) Commissioners Reese Maidlow, and john Deters, CommonPlease Judge F.E. Warren, Sherriff James Ruhe, and Treasurer Edward Heckman.

Courthouse Blueprints Preserved

Recently the original blueprints of the Putnam County's courthouse were found to be deteriorating in the attic of the building. County commissioners entered into an agreement with a government records specialist of the Ohio Historical Society at Bowling Green State University to preserve the historical blueprints, and the 50 pages of original documents were encapsulated between sheets of plastic and bound into a book. The entire project cost only $75 and the blueprints were returned last week to the county. Above commissioners Martin Kuhlman, Alvin Schroeder and Vincent Niese are seen inspecting the blueprints of the building which was constructed in 1912 and 1913 at a cost of $198,290.40.

Inside the Court House, Still the same after 100 years

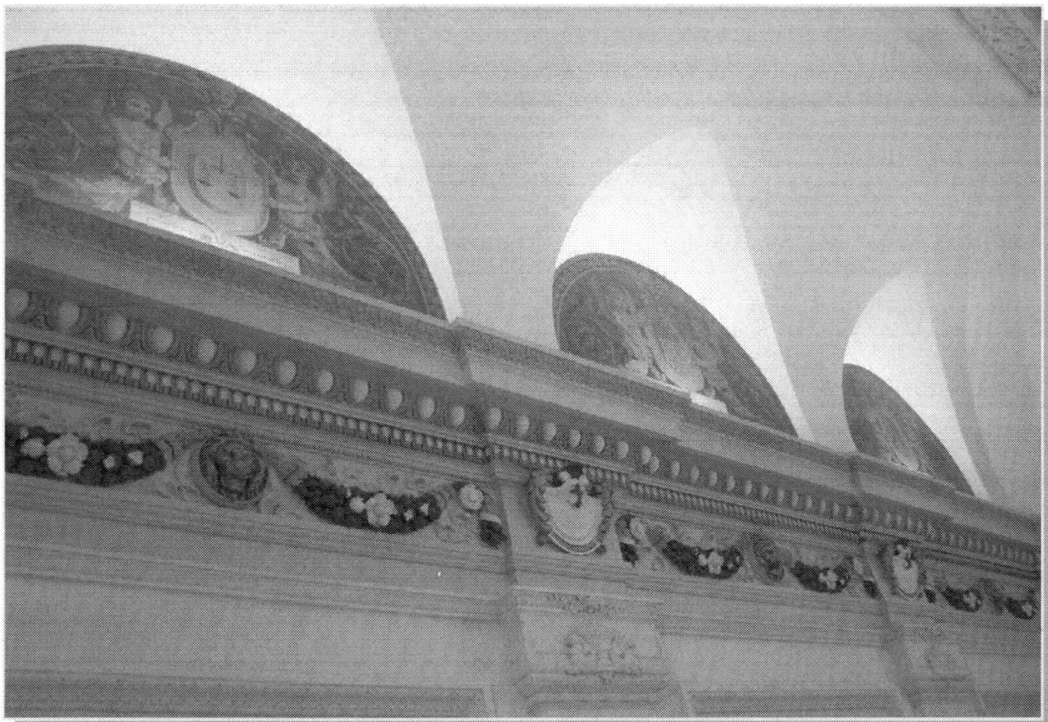

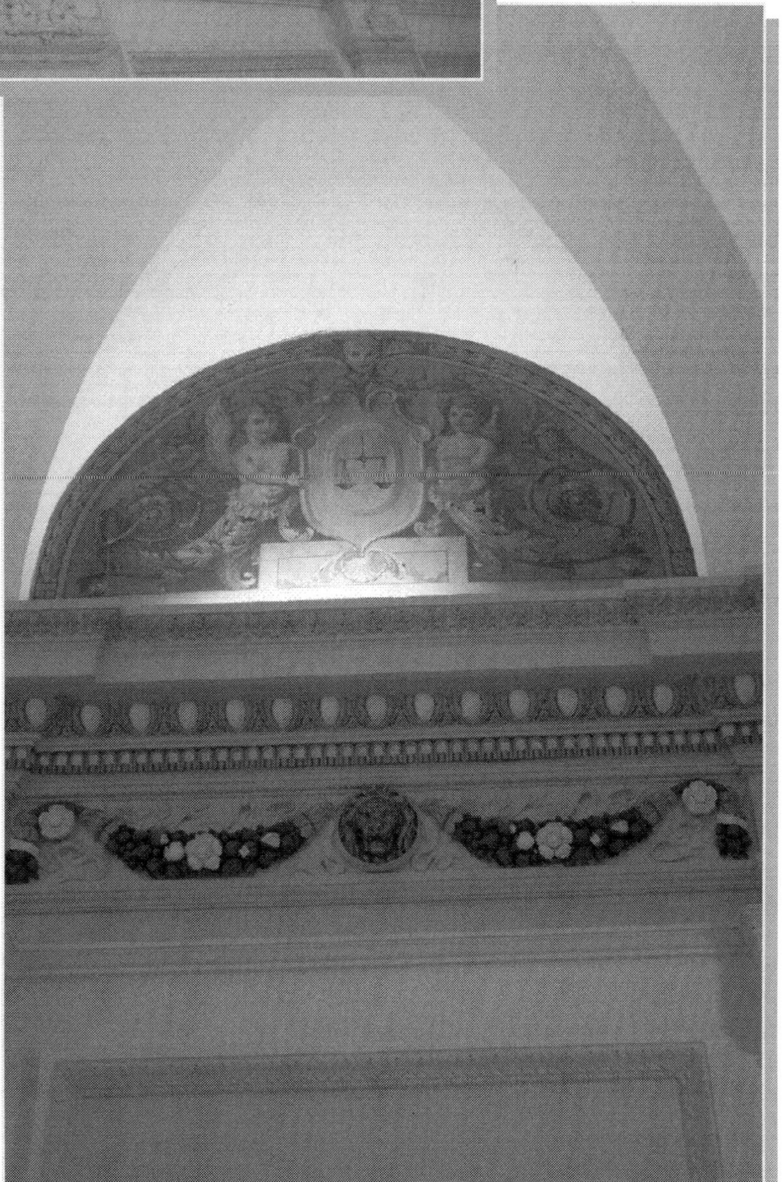

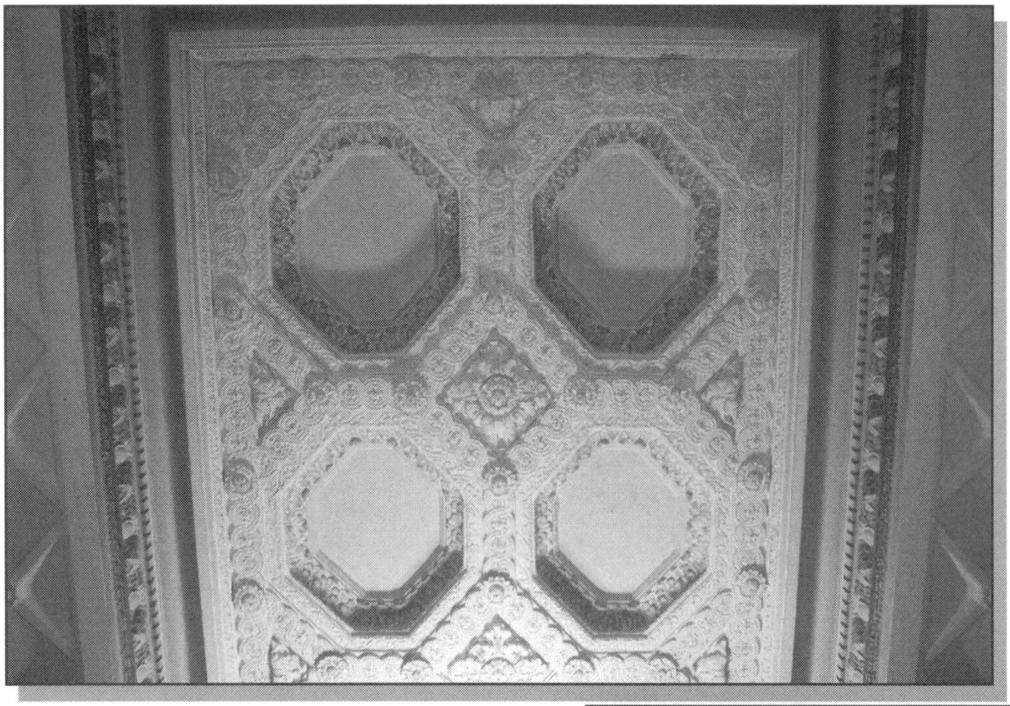

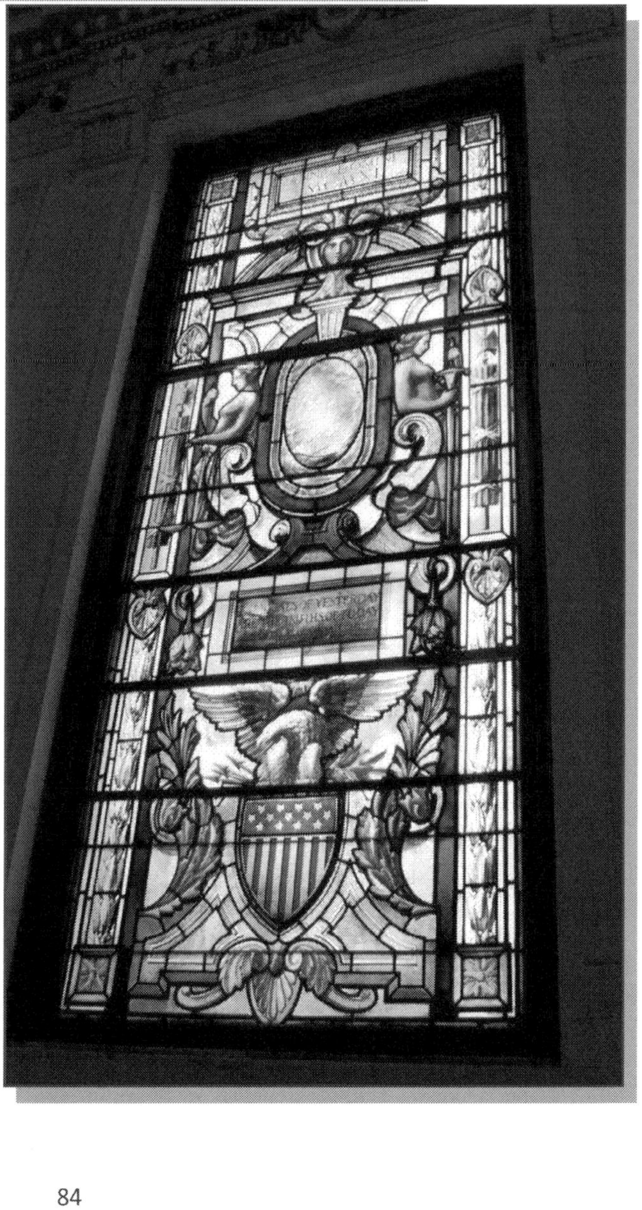

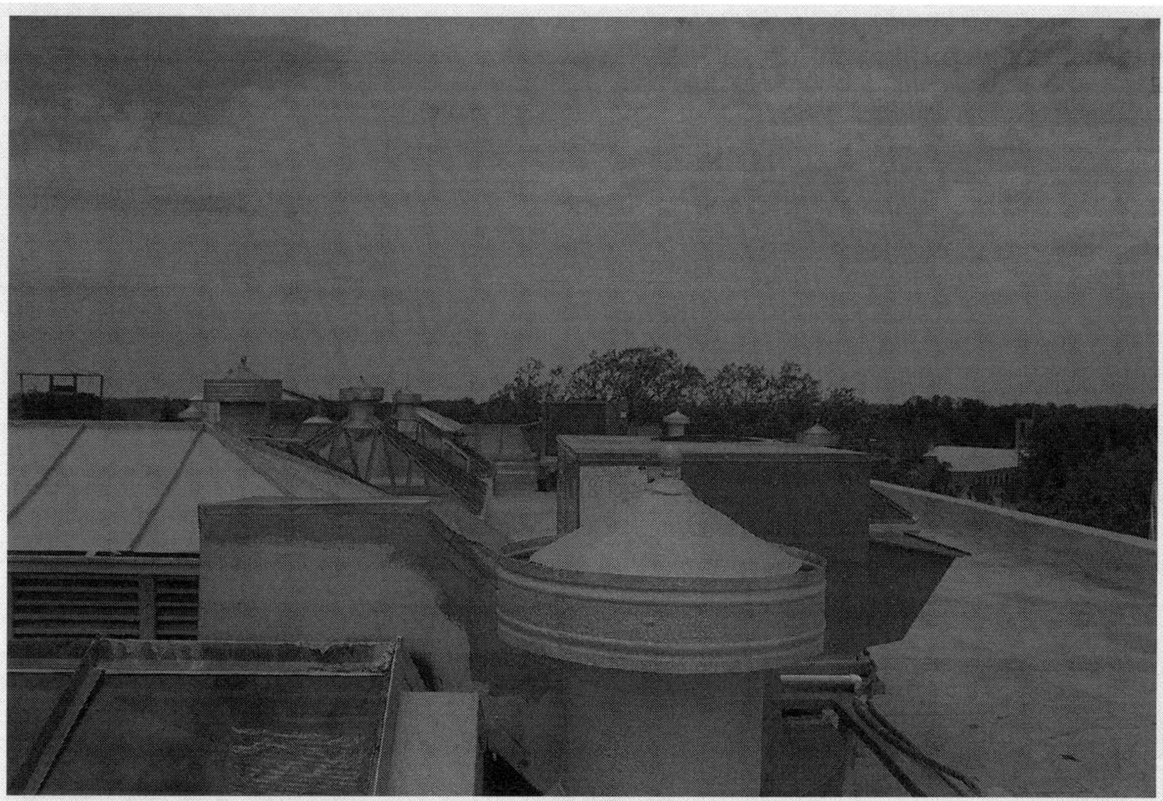

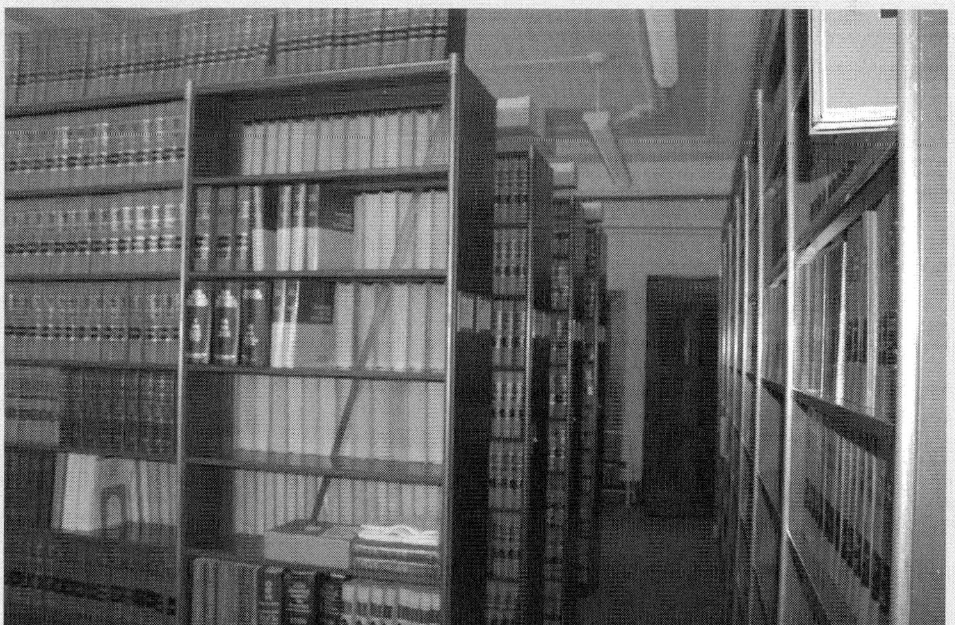

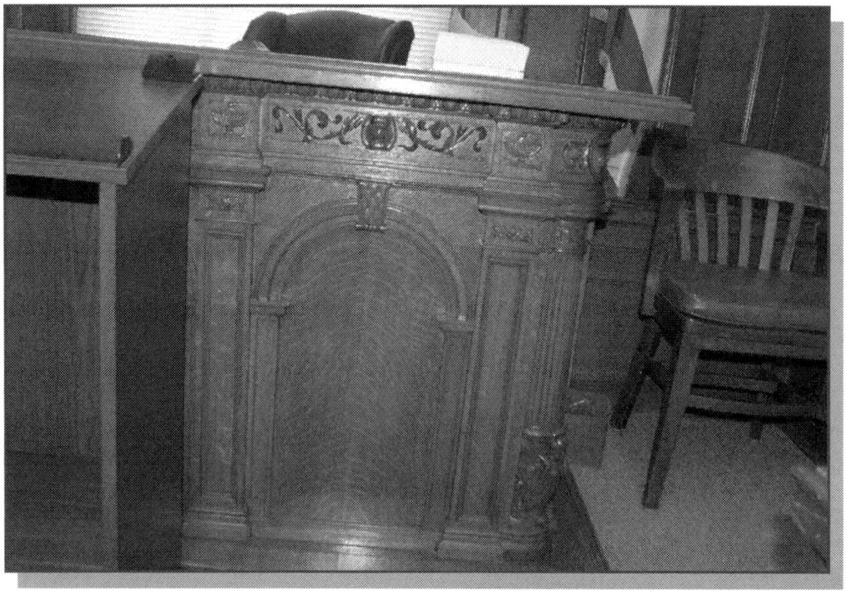

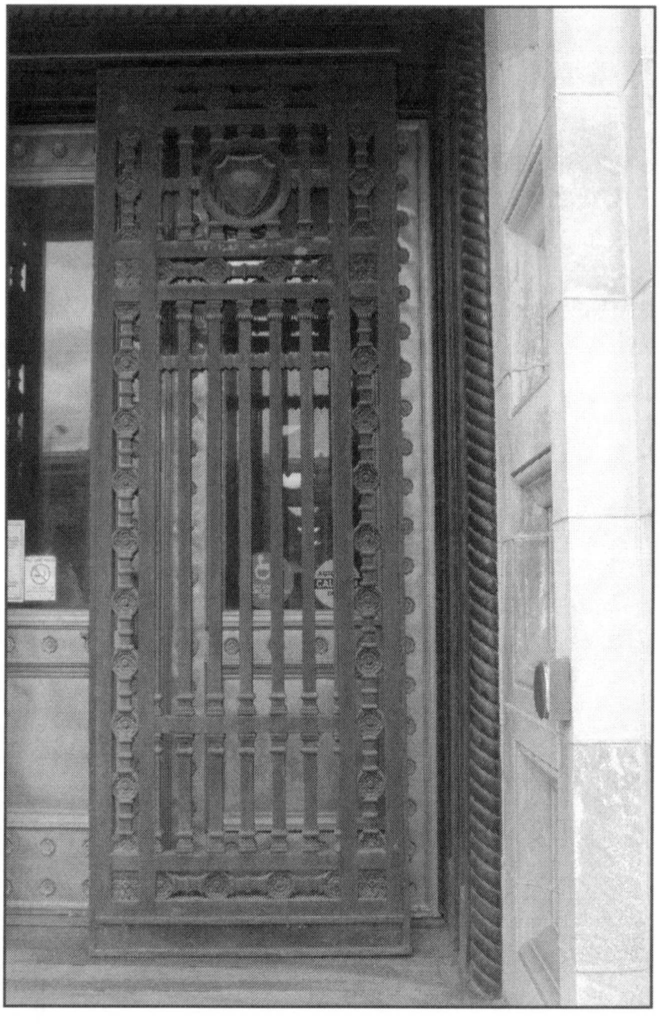

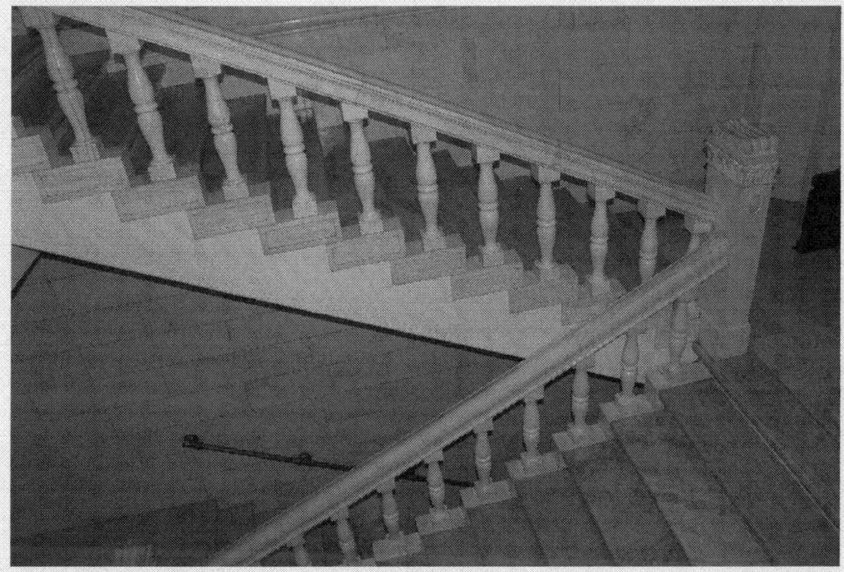

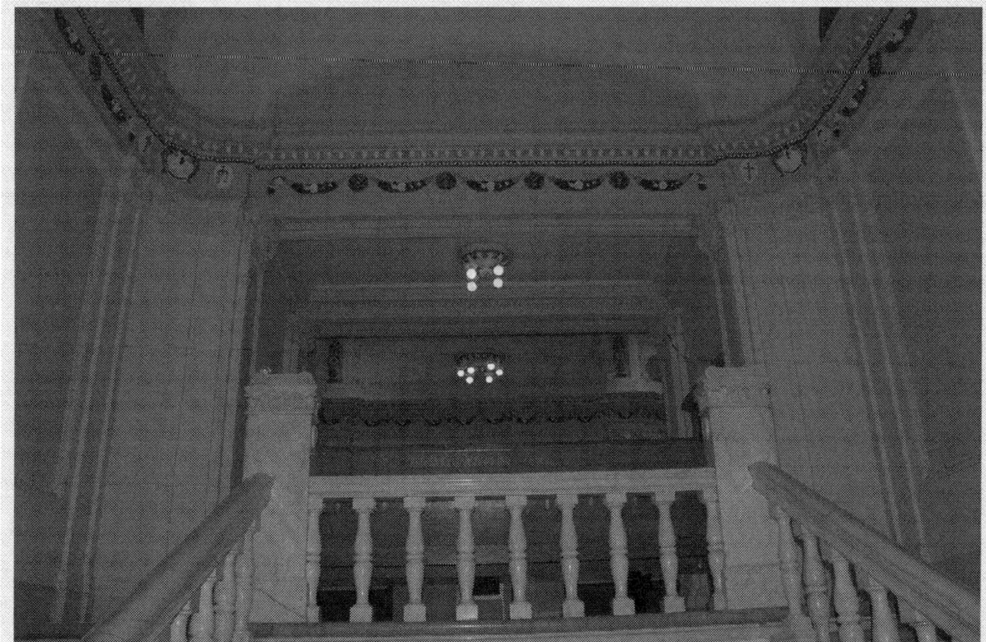

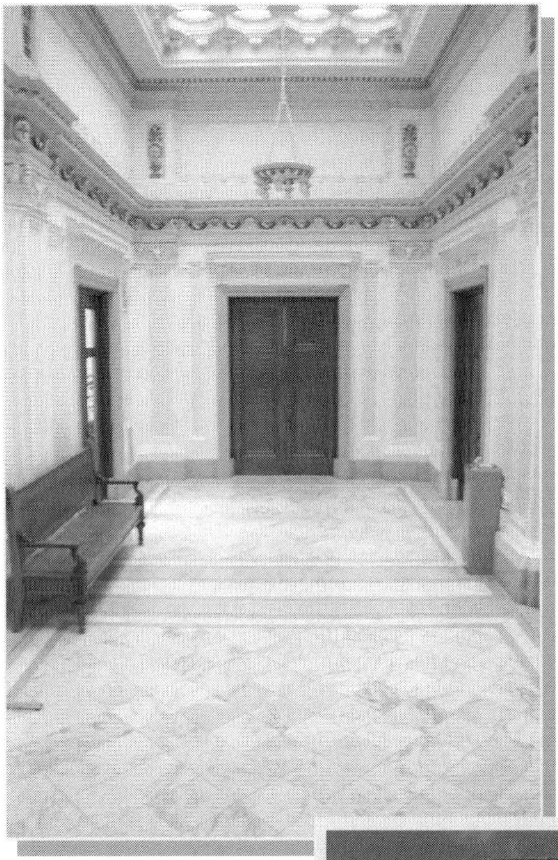

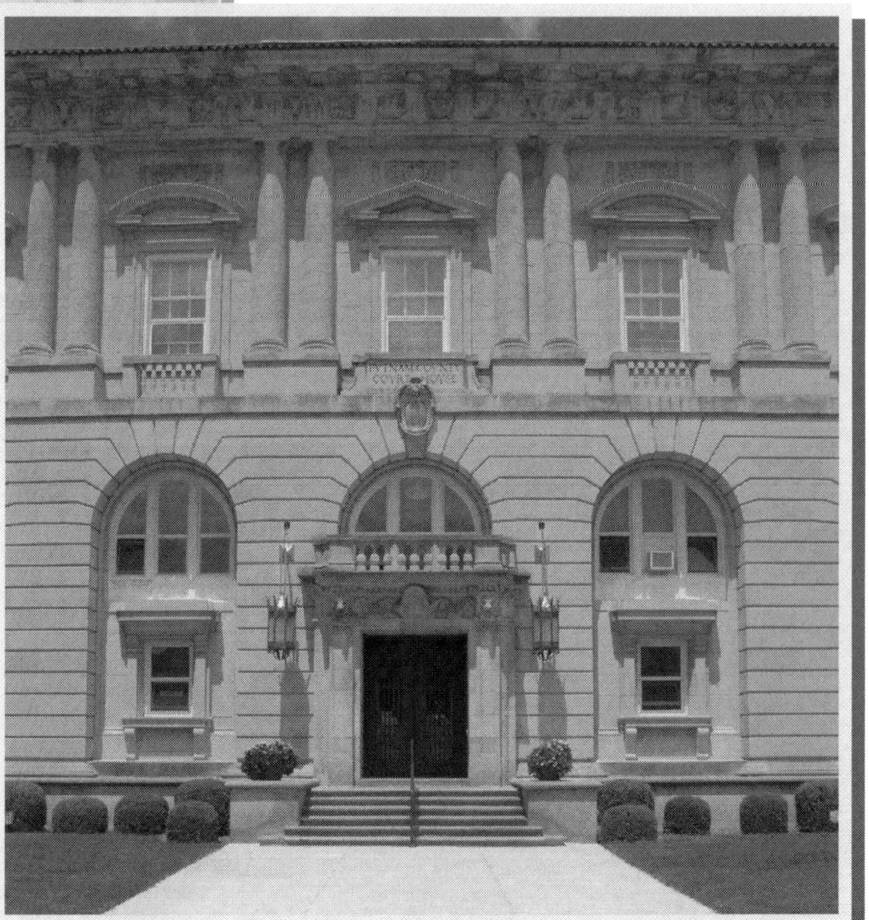

Made in the USA
Columbia, SC
13 September 2022